HOW TO DO
MICROECONOMICS

HANNAH HOLMES

PEARSON

Toronto

Editorial Director: Claudine O'Donnell
Acquisitions Editor: Megan Farrell
Marketing Manager: Loula March
Program Manager: Patricia Ciardullo
Project Manager: Jessica Mifsud
Manager of Content Development: Suzanne Schaan
Developmental Editor: Daniella Balabuk
Production Services: Cenveo® Publisher Service
Permissions Project Manager: Joanne Tang
Photo and Text Permissions Research: Integra
Art Director: Alex Li
Interior and Cover Designer: Anthony Leung
Cover Image: Courtesy of Hannah Holmes

Vice-President, Cross Media and Publishing Services: Gary Bennett

10 9 8 7 6 5 4 3 2 1

Library and Archives Canada Cataloguing in Publication

Holmes, Hannah (Hannah M.), author
    How to do microeconomics / Hannah Holmes.— First Canadian edition.

Includes bibliographical references and index.
ISBN 978-0-13-447633-9 (paperback)

    1. Microeconomics—Textbooks. I. Title. II. Title: Microeconomics.

HB172.H66 2016   338.5   C2016-900243-8

ISBN 978-0-13-447633-9

Brief Table of Contents

Detailed Contents

Preface

I wrote this book because after twenty years of teaching, I have come to a few conclusions. Most students take my principles of microeconomics course because they have to take it as a required course for another major or because they perceive it to be an easy elective, often having taken economics in secondary school. Very few of my 2400 first-year students will go on to take a degree in economics despite my best efforts to convince them that it's a good road to travel. Alas, the majority of my students have only one goal in mind: an A in the course, and nothing short will suffice. Most don't want to really, deeply understand microeconomics; they just want to learn how to "do it" enough to get that elusive A grade. Hence the title and applied problems-based, workbook-style focus of this book.

Year after year, students have asked me if they really need to buy the assigned textbook because they heard from their friends who took my course last year (you know the ones) that they didn't read the book, let alone even open it. I'm hoping those students will open this book. The written, "teachy" material is minimized (I leave it up to all the wonderful instructors out there to elaborate on the theory) while I stress problem solving using—gasp—equations and algebra! Curiously, many students have told me that they didn't really understand the concepts until they did the math and saw the outcomes. Hmm. And, hopefully, the students who understand the theory will find the problems pertinent and reinforcing of those principles presented in class.

Many of the problems go beyond what is usually considered first-year level material, so instructors may choose to use some of the content judiciously. I have found that students today are surprisingly sophisticated and don't want to take my word that producer surplus and profit when there are fixed costs are not the same or that the slope of an indifference curve is MUx/MUy. They want a more substantial explanation so I have provided one (I treat it as optional material in my classes to avoid terrifying the mathematically timid students).

You may notice that there are no boxes with "current events" or "real-world examples" of "microeconomic theory at work." Real-life examples are much more interesting when an instructor puts their own spin on them in lecture. Students are more likely to think that economics is a cool, relevant subject if their professor makes it cool in class, rather than reading about it. Plus, by the time the book gets into the hands of the reader, most current events are anything but. This being said, I defer to instructors to paste a photo of Sidney Crosby into their PowerPoint slides if they so desire.

Speaking of photos, in case you're wondering how the cover of this workbook could possibly relate to microeconomics, think "consumer." Here's a man (who happens to be my hubby) who has made the economic decision based on his opportunity cost to mow his own lawn. He allocated part of his income to purchasing that lawn mower based on his preferences, his budget and the price of the lawn mower. The lawn mower was produced by a firm in order to generate profit. Production required that scarce capital and labour resources be allocated to the production of the lawn mower instead of to the production of a snow blower (which would be an excellent good for Canadian consumers to purchase, given our typical winters). Plus, by mowing the lawn, he keeps his neighbours happy by presenting a well–cared-for yard that won't hurt their property values by conferring upon them a negative externality. Now if this doesn't make you want to take microeconomics, I don't know what will.

I thoroughly enjoyed writing this book because I love teaching first-year micro. I hope my students will attack the problems with confidence and zeal and master introductory microeconomics to earn that A. I hope my colleagues will embrace the spirit with which it was written and steal some of my approaches. And last but not least, I hope my cat will sit on it because it's the highest thing on the floor.

MyEconLab

The Holmes MyEconLab has been designed and refined with a single purpose in mind: to create those moments of understanding that transform the difficult into the clear and obvious. With homework, quiz, test, and activity options, instructors can manage all their assessment needs in one program.

- All of the end-of-chapter problems are assignable and automatically graded in MyEconLab.
- The Gradebook records each student's performance and time spent on the Tests and Study Plan and generates reports by student or by chapter.

MyEconLab also includes the following features:

Digital Interactives

Digital Interactives immerse students in a fundamental economic principle, helping them to learn actively. They can be presented in class as a visually stimulating, highly engaging lecture tool, and can also be assigned with assessment questions for grading. Digital Interactives are designed for use in traditional, online, and hybrid courses, and many incorporate real-time, as well as data display and analysis tools. To learn more, and for a complete list of digital interactives, visit www.myeconlab.com.

Learning Catalytics

Learning Catalytics is a bring-your-own-device classroom engagement tool that allows instructors to ask students questions utilizing 18 different question types, allowing students to participate in real time during lectures. With Learning Catalytics you can:

- Engage students in real time, using open-ended tasks to probe student understanding.
- Promote student participation using any modern Web-enabled device they already have—laptop, smartphone, or tablet.
- Address misconceptions before students leave the classroom.
- Understand immediately where students are and adjust your lecture accordingly.
- Improve your students' critical thinking skills.
- Engage with and record the participation of every student in your classroom.

Learning Catalytics gives you the flexibility to create your own questions to fit your course exactly or choose from a searchable question library Pearson has created. For more information, visit learningcatalytics.com.

Dynamic Study Modules

Dynamic Study Modules, which focus on key topic areas and are available from within MyEconLab, are an additional way for students to obtain tailored help. These modules work by continuously assessing student performance and activity on discrete topics and provide personalized content in real time to reinforce concepts that target each student's particular strengths and weaknesses.

Each Dynamic Study Module, accessed by computer, smartphone, or tablet, promotes fast learning and long-term retention. Because MyEconLab and Dynamic Study Modules help students stay on track and achieve a higher level of subject-matter mastery, more class time is available for interaction, discussion, collaboration, and exploring applications to current news and events.

Instructors can register, create, and access all of their MyEconLab courses at www.myeconlab.com.

Learning Solutions Managers. Pearson's Learning Solutions Managers work with faculty and campus course designers to ensure that Pearson technology products, assessment tools, and online course materials are tailored to meet your specific needs. This highly qualified team is dedicated to helping schools take full advantage of a wide range of educational resources, by assisting in the integration of a variety of instructional materials and media formats. Your local Pearson Canada sales representative can provide you with more details on this service program.

Pearson eText. Pearson eText gives students access to the text whenever and wherever they have online access to the Internet. eText pages look exactly like the printed text, offering powerful new functionality for students and instructors. Users can create notes, highlight text in different colours, create bookmarks, zoom, click hyperlinked words and phrases to view definitions, and view in single-page or two-page view.

Acknowledgements

To Jerry, Mickey, Wills, and Robin, with love.

I would especially like to thank Aleksandra Gajic for her expertise, comments and suggestions for this book. Her contributions to McMaster's Introductory Economics courses as Instructional Assistant and Sessional Lecturer have been outstanding and inspirational.

About the Author

Hannah Holmes is an Assistant Professor in Economics at McMaster University. She holds a BSc in Mathematics and MA in Politics from Brock University and a MA in Economics from McMaster University. She is an applied microeconomist and specializes in sports economics and the teaching and learning of economics. She has authored articles, both independently and jointly, which have appeared in the *Canadian Journal of Political Science*, *Canadian Journal of Urban Research*, and *Municipal World*. In her spare time, she plays guitar, cooks, spoils two cats, and paints with her husband Jerry. She owns a share in her favourite NFL team, the Green Bay Packers.

CHAPTER 1

Introduction

MAIN CONCEPTS AND DEFINITIONS

Economics is the study of how society allocates scarce resources to satisfy peoples' unlimited wants.

Resources are anything used to make something else. They are also called **factors of production (FoP)** or **inputs** into production. The four main categories of resources are:

- Labour

- Land

- Capital (physical capital like buildings, machines, technologies, etc.)

- Entrepreneurship (to bring the first three together and actually produce something)

Scarce means that the quantities of resources available at any time are limited in supply. Think of it as: If something has a price on it, it's scarce. If there are only so many available resources at any time, that means you can't make everything that everybody wants at that time. You have to decide how to allocate those resources so that they are used as best as they can be to fulfill what society wants.

Decision making is done by people. We have to believe that people will make the best decisions they can, given the information they have. No one sets out to purposely make a bad decision. We assume that when making decisions, people are acting rationally.

Economic rationality means people use the information they have to make the best decisions for themselves. For instance, consumers decide what and how much to purchase to get the greatest satisfaction out of their purchases. Firms decide what, how, and how much to produce to make the greatest profit. Everybody acts in their own self-interest.

Here's the catch: The information people have to inform their decisions is not always complete or completely accurate. **Perfect information** means that everyone knows everything they need to know with certainty. There would be no risks involved in making any decision. However, it's not that easy. There's usually some uncertainty, some risk in making decisions. In reality, we often are faced with **asymmetric information**—someone knows something somebody else doesn't know. Think of someone selling a used car on Kijiji who knows whether a vehicle has been in an accident; but the potential buyer may not. That information would probably change a buyer's decision about the purchase.

How do economically rational people make decisions? They think **at the margin**. They don't think, "What if I eat 10 more pieces of pizza?" or "What if our firm produces 2434 more calculators this week?" Instead, they think, "What if I eat *one* more piece of pizza—what would that add to my satisfaction from my entire pizza meal?" or "What if we produce *one* more calculator—what would that add to our total weekly profit?" Marginal thinking means thinking incrementally, in terms of doing *one* more of something.

Consider a calculator firm. Suppose it is producing 2021 calculators. Someone in management then realizes that the company is not producing enough—it could produce more and see an increase in profit. What's the magic number of calculators? Someone could suggest that they increase production to 2434 calculators, but then they realize that's too many and the company is actually losing money. If they had thought about increasing production by one calculator at a time, eventually they would have landed on the perfect quantity. By making a big change in production, they missed the profit-maximizing number of calculators. When you think marginally, you'll come to the best decision given the information you have.

Making decisions also means that you have to make choices. Because there's scarcity, you'll have to give up something in order to get something else. What's one of (if not the most) scarcest resources? It's time. Every hour you spend watching TV is an hour you don't spend studying for your economics test. To watch one hour of TV you give up one hour of study time. This is an example of an opportunity cost.

Opportunity cost is the cost of everything you give up to get something else. Using our example, the opportunity cost of one hour of TV is one hour of study time. Think of opportunity cost as:

- To get <u>1</u> of something, you give up (<u>a specific quantity</u>) of something else.

What do we mean by "something else?" When you decided to watch TV for an hour, there were probably many other things you could have done in that hour besides studying for your test. You could have played a video game, gone out for a coffee with friends, cleaned your room . . . the list of alternatives could be huge. What we do is consider the **best forgone alternative**: Which of the things you gave up had the greatest value? Hopefully it was the hour of study time.

Here's an example. You buy a ticket to a Toronto Maple Leafs' hockey game for $250 for Saturday night. Your friend will drive so you don't have any other financial costs to worry about. Instead, you could have attended a Hamilton Ti-Cats game for $60, or gone out for chicken wings for $40, or worked your shift bartending at the Sheraton for a wedding where you could have made $400 in wages and tips. Your opportunity cost of going to the Leafs' game is what you spent on the ticket—$250—plus the value of the *best* forgone alternative—the $400 from bartending which you won't get. Your total opportunity cost of going to the Leafs' game is therefore $650. Hopefully the Leafs win.

The money you paid for the ticket is an **explicit cost**. You actually had to pay out some money to get the ticket and you got a receipt for it. The lost wages from not working are an **implicit cost**. You gave up that income but you didn't have to spend any money out of pocket; there's no record for hours you didn't work, no receipts. So, opportunity cost includes explicit and implicit costs.

Attending the Leafs' game required you to use up some of your resources. You had to use up some money resources to buy the ticket plus some time resources to get there, watch the game, and get home. Was this the best use of your resources? In economics, we always question whether we, as a society, use our scarce resources as best as they can be used. If the answer is yes, we say we are using our resources **efficiently**. We don't want to waste any resources because they are scarce, but sometimes it happens.

One way we measure whether we're using our resources efficiently is by examining what's going on in the market. A **market** is the coming together of buyers and sellers to buy and sell goods and services. It doesn't have to be a physical place—think of eBay, the world's largest marketplace, or a stock market where much trading takes place online. Any time you have buyers buying and sellers selling, you have a market.

There are different ways to think about markets. You can think about a market for a specific good or service, like the market for SUVs or the market for haircuts. You can think about a market for the resources used to produce the goods and services which get sold to consumers, like the market for steel or the market for hair stylists.

You can even think about markets at an economy-wide level. In capitalist countries, we usually think of **free markets** where all decision-making is decentralized. This means consumers decide what and how much they want to buy and firms decide what and how much they want to produce and sell. There's no government authority telling buyers or sellers what they can do (as long as what consumers and sellers are doing is legal and doesn't hurt anyone). Remember the former USSR? That was a **centrally planned economy** or command economy where a central authority (government) dictated how resources would be allocated for production and consumption; many industries were government owned. Canada is a **mixed economy**: we are mostly a free market but we do have some industries that are government owned (GO Transit, owned by the province of Ontario, is an example).

You can also think about different market *structures* within an economy. Are many smaller firms all selling identical goods at the same price? Is just one firm selling a good that no one else produces? Something in between? These are questions we explore in microeconomics.

Microeconomics (our course) deals with decision making at the individual level. We study how households—you and me—and individual firms make economic decisions about consumption and production. **Macroeconomics** looks at economy-wide phenomena like unemployment, interest rates, inflation, and aggregate (economy-wide) output and demand.

Both fields of economics rely on the use of **models** to help explain or predict economic outcomes. Models can explain how an economy works. They can be used to predict what would happen in a market or in an entire economy if some economic factor changed.

Essentially, economists try to model human behaviour, a very complex thing to try to predict accurately in any discipline. We have to make assumptions about how consumers and firms react to changes in order to keep our models simple enough to tell us something meaningful. These aren't wild assumptions; they are based on theory. A good model will give good predictions that policy makers can use to implement sound economic policies.

Any economic policy involves two levels of economic understanding. **Positive economics** tells it the way it is, the way the world actually works. Policy makers need to know that if they do such-and-such, then such-and-such will result. **Normative economics** points at what should be, how things ought to be. This is where policy makers, using their own judgments, decide what should happen, based on their opinions and what economists predict will happen for various options they might choose.

Here's an example: The province is thinking about increasing minimum wage rates again. Positive economic analysis shows that if wages increase, employers will want to reduce the number of workers they hire (because now it will cost too much to employ so many people) and unemployment will increase. Policymakers have to weigh the increase in unemployment against their normative belief that low-wage earners should be paid more to improve their standard of living. If the benefit to society of a higher minimum wage outweighs the cost of having higher unemployment, the minimum wage should increase.

A SIMPLE MODEL OF THE ECONOMY

Consider an economy that trades with the rest of the world and has a government which collects taxes and spends money as well as makes transfer payments (like employment insurance benefits or child-care benefits) to some people. There is also a financial sector where banks hold peoples' savings and make loans to firms. In this economy households provide resources (like their labour) to firms to produce goods and services and earn income to spend on those goods and services. Firms hire factors of production in the resource market and pay them to make goods and services which they sell in the product market.

We have two flows happening in this economy. One is the **flow of income**—how money moves through the economy. At the same time there is a **flow of goods and services**—how actual products move through the economy. On the diagram "G & S" is short for "goods and services." The flow of income is illustrated by the red line and the flow of goods and services is illustrated by the grey line.

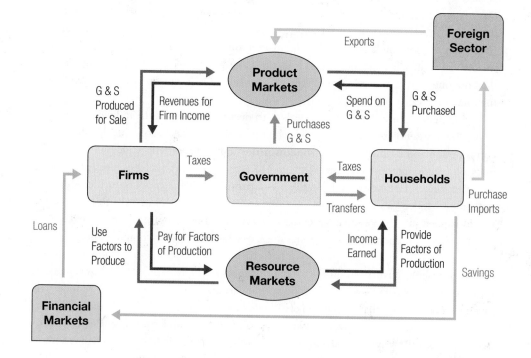

This is a simple model. There are other flows not included in the diagram to keep it from becoming cluttered and too hard to follow. For example, we left out the investment flow where firms receive capital investments. Hopefully you will get an idea of how the economy works.

KEY TERMS

economics

resources

factors of production (FoP)

inputs

scarce

economic rationality

perfect information

asymmetric information

at the margin

opportunity cost

best forgone alternative

explicit cost

implicit cost

efficiently

market

free markets

centrally planned economy

mixed economy

microeconomics

macroeconomics

models

positive economics

normative economics

flow of income

flow of goods and services

SOLVED EXAMPLE PROBLEMS

As you can tell, not much is going on in this chapter. Just a few problems to work through.

1. Which of these statements are normative and which are positive?

   a) The government should raise sales taxes if it wants to pay down the debt.

   This is normative: The "should" is the speaker's judgment.

   b) Canada would be better off if the government revisited its budget for education.

   This is normative: "Would be better off" is an opinion lacking any factual support.

   c) The unemployment rate was down in part due to a 2% surge in the service sector.

   This is positive: just a statement which tells it like it is.

2. Suppose you have 3 hours of free time when you can either play a video game or watch 2 movies you downloaded. What's the opportunity cost of playing a video game?

   Opportunity cost is what you give up of one good or activity to get or do some of another. If you play a video game, you give up watching 2 movies, so the opportunity cost of playing a game is watching 2 movies.

PROBLEMS

1. You are deciding between two vacation packages. Package A is all-inclusive. Package B includes your flight and accommodations, but food and beverages are out-of-pocket expenses for you. What is the opportunity cost of Package B in terms of Package A?

2. A baker has 20 minutes left in her shift. She can bake either 4 dozen cookies or 2 dozen muffins.

    a) What is the opportunity cost of 1 dozen cookies in terms of muffins?

    b) What is the opportunity cost of 1 dozen muffins in terms of cookies?

3. There's a saying that "There's no such thing as a free lunch." Can you explain the meaning of this statement as an economist might?

SOLUTIONS

1. You are deciding between two vacation packages. Package A is all-inclusive. Package B includes your flight and accommodations, but food and beverages are out-of-pocket expenses for you. What is the opportunity cost of Package B in terms of Package A?

   If you said the cost of food and beverages, in the absence of any detailed costs you'd be wrong. Package A probably costs more because it includes the costs of food and beverages, but you have no way of knowing without dollar amounts. Package B might actually be cheaper in total.

2. A baker has 20 minutes left in her shift. She can bake either 4 dozen cookies or 2 dozen muffins.

   a) What is the opportunity cost of <u>1</u> dozen cookies in terms of muffins?

   To get 4 dozen cookies, she gives up 2 dozen muffins.

   To get 1 dozen cookies, she gives up 2/4 = 1/2 dozen muffins.

   The opportunity cost of 1 dozen cookies is 1/2 dozen muffins.

   b) What is the opportunity cost of <u>1</u> dozen muffins in terms of cookies?

   To get 2 dozen muffins, she gives up 4 dozen cookies.

   To get 1 dozen muffins, she gives up 4/2 = 2 dozen cookies.

   The opportunity cost of 1 dozen muffins is 2 dozen cookies.

   (Notice that this is the inverse of the opportunity cost of cookies in part a.)

3. There's a saying that "There's no such thing as a free lunch." Can you explain the meaning of this statement as an economist might?

   Even if you don't have to put out any money for lunch, there's an opportunity cost: You could have used the time you spent having that free lunch doing something else. You give up another activity to get the lunch.

CHAPTER 2

Production Possibilities and Gains from Trade

MAIN CONCEPTS AND DEFINITIONS

Suppose we take a snapshot of an economy, freezing it at a moment in time. At that moment, there are only so many resources available to produce goods and services and that's that. We call that the economy's **resource endowment**. It's a list of all available resources an economy has at any given time. Producers have a technology to produce their goods and services, and that's the technology they have to use, period. We are taking the resource endowment and current technology as given—it is what it is.

We want to determine: What is the best the economy can do in terms of how much it can produce, given its resource endowment and technology? Let's see what the possibilities are and graph combinations of goods that can be produced when the economy is using all of its resources and its current technology. To graph these combinations, we can only have two "goods"—one for each axis. Of course, economies produce more than just two goods; let's really make it simple and suppose an economy just produces two goods.

The graph of the different combinations of goods an economy can produce using all its resources efficiently given its current technology is called a **production possibilities frontier, PPF** for short. It shows the best an economy can do at the moment the snapshot was taken.

Now, we have defined the "best" as the economy using all its resources efficiently. That means every member of the labour force is working and working fully (no unemployment, no slackers), there are no machines or other available equipment that are sitting idle, no productive land being under-utilized … you get the picture. This implies that if we're producing X amount of Good A and Y amount of Good B, in order to produce more of Good A we have to give up some of Good B; we don't have any extra resources (we're already using them all) so to produce more of Good A we have to take away some resources from the production of Good B which means fewer Good Bs.

The PPF therefore will show **opportunity costs**—how much of one good we have to give up to produce more of the other good. It's time for an example.

EXAMPLE: WESTDALE

Westdale can produce two goods: smartphones and trucks. The following table shows just four combinations of phones and trucks that Westdale can produce if it uses all its resources efficiently given its currently technology.

	Phones	Trucks
A	8000	0
B	6000	500
C	5000	700
D	0	1100

If Westdale devotes all its resources to producing only smartphones, it can produce 8000 phones but 0 trucks. If it wants to produce 500 trucks, it has to take some resources away from the phone sector to make those trucks; it gives up 2000 phones (goes from 8000 to 6000 phones) to get those 500 trucks. If it wants to produce 700 trucks, it has to move more resources from the phone sector and loses another 1000 phones (down to 5000 phones from 6000). If it wants to focus on producing only trucks, it will use all its resources for trucks and can't make any phones (it loses 5000 phones to pick up another 400 trucks for a total of 1100 trucks).

Let's graph these combinations. We can approximate the combinations in between by joining up our 4 points with a curve to get a PPF:

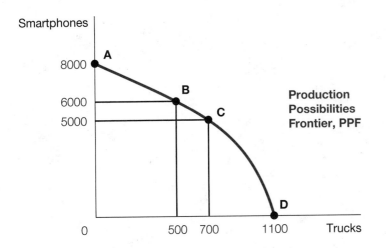

Every point on the PPF is efficient—Westdale is using all its resources given its technology. It doesn't necessarily mean they're producing the amount *society wants*; it only means that they're producing that combination of goods efficiently.

What about points <u>not</u> on the PPF?

Have a look at the following diagram. Point H, outside the PPF, is unattainable. There are not enough resources, or not the right technology, or no combination of both that would allow Westdale to produce that many of both goods right now. Point K, inside the PPF, is feasible but inefficient. They can produce more of both goods so they must not be using all their resources or their technology to the fullest.

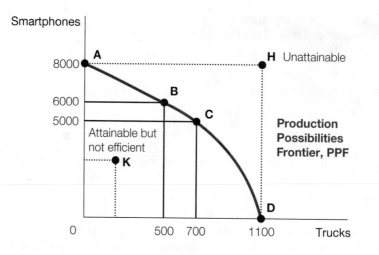

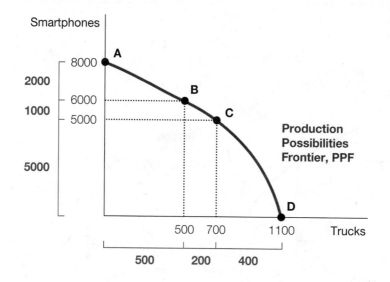

Opportunity costs along the PPF

Moving from A to B: To get 500 trucks, give up 2000 phones.
To get 1 truck, give up $2000/500 = 4$ phones.
The opportunity cost of a truck is 4 phones, moving from A to B.

Moving from B to C: To get 200 trucks, give up 1000 phones.
To get 1 truck, give up $1000/200 = 5$ phones.
The opportunity cost of a truck is 5 phones, moving from B to C.

Moving from C to D: To get 400 trucks, give up 5000 phones.
To get 1 truck, give up $5000/400 = 12.5$ phones.
The opportunity cost of a truck is 12.5 phones, moving from C to D.

Notice that the opportunity cost of a truck increases as we move down Westdale's PPF.

Increasing opportunity costs explain why the PPF is bowed out. The more trucks we want, the more expensive they become in terms of the number of smartphones we have to give up. When we first start shifting resources from the phone sector to the truck sector, we move our least productive phone-making resources first, so we don't lose too many phones. The more and more trucks we want, the more and more we pull resources from the phone sector and now we are pulling our really productive phone-making resources; we now lose a lot of phones to get more trucks.

The |**slope**| **of a PPF** is the opportunity cost of the good on the horizontal axis (on the X-axis). Always.

We can easily calculate the opportunity cost of a smartphone. It is the inverse of the opportunity cost of a truck moving backward over the same range. For example:

Moving from B to A: To get 2000 phones, give up 500 trucks.
To get 1 phone, give up 500/2000 = 0.25 trucks.
This is just 1/4 where 4 is the opportunity cost of a truck moving from A to B.

Can opportunity costs be constant? Yes. It's possible that resources can be **perfectly shiftable** and can be equally productive so that you always give up the same amount of one good to get more of the other. If opportunity costs are constant and are the slope of a PPF, then a PPF with constant opportunity costs must be linear. Only a straight line has a constant slope.

Another point: notice that we consider opportunity costs as how much you have to give up of a good to get <u>one</u> of another. This makes it easy to compare opportunity costs of goods for different producers.

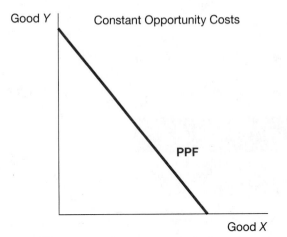

Shifts in the PPF

After some time passes, it is possible that things may have changed in an economy and we can take a new snapshot of what's going on. Anything that changes the available resources (the quantity of resources or how productive they are) or changes the current technology will shift the PPF. A rightward shift of the curve signals **economic growth**. This could be caused by immigration that increases the labour force, the development of a new technology that makes workers more productive, an increase in land converted for industrial development and so forth. A leftward shift signals **economic contraction**. This could be caused by an event that reduces the amount of productive resources available, like a natural disaster or mass emigration of labour resources.

COMPARATIVE ADVANTAGE AND GAINS FROM TRADE

Let's put opportunity costs to work and go straight to an example.

EXAMPLE: TONY AND DENNY

Suppose there are two people trapped on an island: Tony the tailor and Denny the diner-owner. Two goods are produced—clothes and food—and both our islanders can produce each good. We have a table that reports how much of each good they can produce if they produce <u>only one or the other</u>.

	Clothes	or	Food	Hours to Produce
Tony	28		14	8
Denny	30		120	8

Let's compute their opportunity costs.

For Tony: To get 14 food, give up 28 clothes.

To get 1 food, give up $28/14 = 2$ clothes.

The opportunity cost of a food = 2 clothes.

The opportunity cost of a clothes = 1/2 food.

For Denny: To get 120 food, give up 30 clothes.

To get 1 food, give up $30/120 = 1/4$ clothes.

The opportunity cost of a food = 1/4 clothes.

The opportunity cost of a clothes = 4 food.

Now let's make a nice table of their opportunity costs:

	Opportunity Costs of Clothes	Opportunity Costs of Food
Tony	1/2 food	2 clothes
Denny	4 food	1/4 clothes

Comparative Advantage: Someone has a comparative advantage if he or she can produce a good at a lower opportunity cost than anyone else. Whoever has a comparative advantage should **specialize** in the production of that good (produce only that good and zero of the other good[1]) and trade.

Tony can produce clothes at a lower opportunity cost than Denny (Tony gives up 1/2 food compared to Denny's 4 food). Tony has a comparative advantage in the production of clothes. He should specialize in the production of clothes and trade with Denny to get food.

---

[1] In reality, economies wouldn't produce just the good in which they had comparative advantage. They'd produce some of the other good, too. However, they would likely produce more of the comparative-advantage good than needed for domestic consumption and export the rest to other economies.

Denny can produce food at a lower opportunity cost than Tony (Denny gives up 1/4 clothes compared to Tony's 2 clothes). Denny has a comparative advantage in the production of food. He should specialize in the production of food and trade with Tony to get clothes.

Suppose we're told that before Tony and Denny met up, Tony produced and consumed 7 food and 14 clothes and Denny produced and consumed 90 food and 10 clothes. Here's what it looks like on their PPFs:

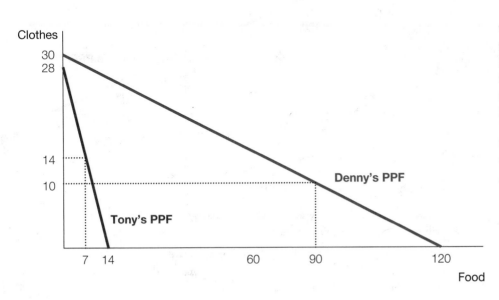

We have no idea what these PPFs really look like because we only have two quantity values. For simplicity, we assume it's a linear PPF. To graph each PPF, just plot each of the two values you are given on the appropriate axis and join them up.

Now Tony and Denny meet up and decide to trade with each other. They agree on a price of 13 food for 13 clothes. Here's how the deal went down:

	Tony		Denny	
	Clothes	Food	Clothes	Food
Without Trade				
Produce and Consume	14	7	10	90
With Trade				
Produce	28	0	0	120
Trade	−13	+13	+13	−13
Consume	15	13	13	107
Gain	+1	+6	+3	+17

Tony and Denny both gained from trade. By specializing in the production of the good in which they had comparative advantage, they were able to trade with each other and end up consuming more of both goods than they could when they were on their own. Both experienced **gains from trade**.

Let's draw their consumption after trade has occurred:

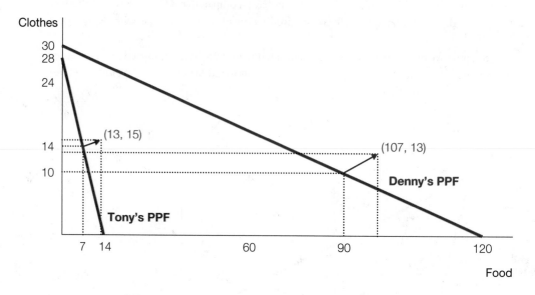

Two things:

1. If no one has comparative advantage (they have the same opportunity costs) there will be no trade (no gains to be made).

2. If someone (a person, a country) has a comparative advantage in one good, the other (person, country) necessarily has a comparative advantage in the other good (mathematically it has to be so).

Determining terms of trade (prices)

For Denny to "sell" food to Tony, he has to get more than what it costs him to produce it: he has to get more than 1/4 clothes. For Tony to "buy" food from Denny, he has to pay less than what it costs him to produce it himself: He has to pay less than 2 clothes.

The price of 1 food = 1 clothes satisfies both conditions (any price between 1/4 and 2 clothes would do it).

That's why they settled on 13 food = 13 clothes which is the same as 1 food = 1 clothes.

ABSOLUTE ADVANTAGE

Absolute advantage: If you are more productive than anyone else, you have an absolute advantage in the production of that good.

Absolute advantage and comparative advantage are two different concepts. Comparative advantage is based on opportunity costs; absolute advantage is based on productivity.

Productivity: You are more productive than someone else if you can produce a greater quantity of a good using the same quantity of resources as someone else. Alternatively, you will be more productive than someone else if you can produce the same amount as someone else but use fewer resources.

An easy formula to calculate productivity is:

(amount of output)/(amount of inputs used)

EXAMPLE: TONY AND DENNY

The only input into production for either of them is time.

For Tony: Productivity for clothes is 28/8 = 3.5 clothes per hour.
              Productivity for food is 14/8 = 1.75 food per hour.
For Denny: Productivity for clothes is 30/8 = 3.75 clothes per hour.
              Productivity for food is 120/8 = 15 food per hour.

In one hour, Denny can produce more clothes and more food than Tony. Denny is more productive in the production of both goods so Denny has an absolute advantage in the production of both goods.

Even though Tony has a comparative advantage in clothes, he is less productive than Denny in both goods. However, the decision to trade is based on comparative advantage, not absolute advantage. As long as comparative advantage exists, there are gains to be made from trade.

ANOTHER EXAMPLE: CANADA AND THE US

Canada and the US can each produce hockey players and basketball players. The only resource they each use is the number of years of training. Here's the table of how many players they can produce if they produce only one kind of player or the other in the time reported:

	Hockey Players	Basketball Players	Years to Produce
Canada	200	32	8
US	256	240	8

For Canada: Productivity for hockey players is 200/8 = 25 per year.
              Productivity for basketball players is 32/8 = 4 per year.
For the US: Productivity for hockey players is 256/8 = 32 per year.
              Productivity for basketball players is 240/8 = 30 per year.

In one year, the US can produce more hockey players and basketball players than Canada. The US is more productive in the production of both sports' players and has an absolute advantage in the production of both hockey players and basketball players.

Should the US produce and trade both kinds of players to Canada? Knowing who has an absolute advantage won't help us decide whether trade should take place. Remember from our first example that the decision to trade is based on comparative advantage, not absolute advantage.

Let's calculate each country's opportunity costs to see whether any country has a comparative advantage.

For Canada: To get 32 basketball players, give up 200 hockey players.
To get 1 basketball player, give up 6.25 hockey players.
The opportunity cost of a basketball player is 6.25 hockey players.
The opportunity cost of a hockey player is 0.16 basketball players.

For the US: To get 240 basketball players, give up 256 hockey players.
To get 1 basketball player, give up 1.07 hockey players.
The opportunity cost of a basketball player is 1.07 hockey players.
The opportunity cost of a hockey player is 0.94 basketball players.

Canada has comparative advantage in the production of hockey players and should specialize in and trade hockey players to the US. The US has comparative advantage in the production of basketball players and should specialize in and trade basketball players to Canada. Both countries would enjoy gains from trade, even though the US has an absolute advantage in the production of both kinds of players.

KEY TERMS

resource endowment

production possibilities frontier (PPF)

opportunity costs

increasing opportunity costs

|slope| of a PPF

perfectly shiftable

economic growth

economic contraction

comparative advantage

specialize

gains from trade

absolute advantage

productivity

SOLVED EXAMPLE PROBLEMS

1. Illustrate what happens to the PPF for Westdale in each of the following scenarios.

    a) A severe flu season keeps a substantial number of workers away from their jobs in both the smartphone and truck sectors.

Not all resources—workers—are producing to their fullest capacity. This means Westdale is producing at a point inside the PPF. Once the workers get better and return to work, Westdale will be back at a point on the PPF. The PPF doesn't shift in this case because the endowment of workers did not change.

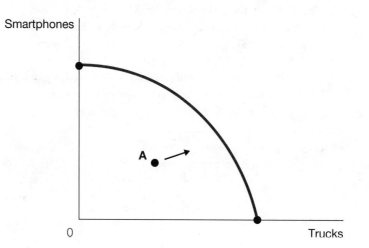

b) A new smartphone technology results in faster production of a smartphone but doesn't help the truck sector in any way.

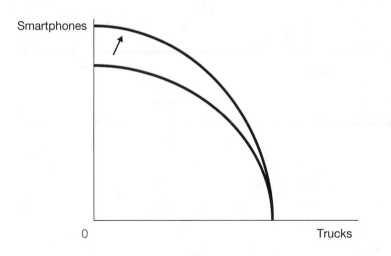

The technology increases productivity in the phone sector; for any number of trucks, Westdale can now produce more phones, too. The PPF rotates up the smartphone axis.

If Westdale uses all its resources to produce phones, it can produce more phones than before. If it uses all its resources to produce trucks, it can still only produce the same number of trucks as before.

c) A new truck plant in Westdale opens and workers from both sectors in Westdale move to take one of the new, high-paying factory jobs.

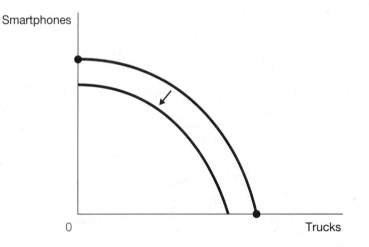

The number of labour resources (workers) in both sectors decreases. The PPF shifts in toward the origin. Fewer resources mean fewer of both goods can now be produced compared to before.

2. The following table depicts the production quantities of capital goods (like machinery and equipment) and consumption goods (final products sold to households) in millions for the economies of Northwood and Southfield when they are using all their resources, given their technology, in one year.

	Capital Goods	Consumption Goods
Northwood	5000	12 000
Southfield	4000	13 000

a) What are the opportunity costs of both goods for both economies? Let's use decimals instead of fractions for a change:

For Northwood:

To get 5000-million capital goods, give up 12 000-million consumption goods.

To get 1 capital good, give up 12 000/5000 = 2.4 consumption goods (the "million" cancels out).

The opportunity cost of a capital good is 2.4 consumption goods.

The opportunity cost of a consumption good is 1/2.4 = 0.42 capital goods.

For Southfield:

To get 4000-million capital goods, give up 13 000-million consumption goods.

To get 1 capital good, give up 13 000/4000 = 3.25 consumption goods (the "million" cancels out again, of course).

The opportunity cost of a capital good is 3.25 consumption goods.

The opportunity cost of a consumption good is 1/3.25 = 0.31 capital goods.

b) Which economies have a comparative advantage in which good (if any)?

Northwood has a lower opportunity cost in capital goods than Southfield (2.4 versus 3.25 consumption goods) so Northwood has a comparative advantage in the production of capital goods and should specialize in and trade capital goods to Southfield.

Southfield has a lower opportunity cost in consumption goods than Northwood (0.31 versus 0.42 capital goods), so Southfield has a comparative advantage in the production of consumption goods and should specialize in and trade consumption goods to Southfield.

c) Northwood is willing to trade capital goods to Southfield. Which is a possible price that both economies would agree to? 1 consumption good for 1 capital good; 3 consumption goods for 1 capital good; 1 consumption good for 4 capital goods.

Northwood has to get a price for capital goods that is more than it costs them to make and Southfield won't pay a price that is more than what it costs them to make. The price therefore has to be between 2.4 and 3.25 consumption goods for 1 capital good. So, 3 consumption goods for 1 capital good is a realistic price.

d) Does either economy have an absolute advantage in production?

The table reports output for both Northwood and Southfield for one year, so annual productivity for each economy is simply the output stated in the table. We don't have to do a separate calculation of productivity. (Note that productivity doesn't have to be measured at an hourly rate; we can define the time frame any way we choose.)

Therefore, from the table we see that Southfield has absolute advantage in the production of both capital and consumption goods; it can produce more of both goods using the same amount of resources (in this case, one year of the time resource) as Northwood.

e) Suppose Northwood is looking to the future and wants to plan for economic growth in the next 10 years. How could it allocate production to achieve faster, greater economic growth?

Northwood should concentrate on producing capital goods like machinery, equipment, new technological processes, and so on, which increase its resource endowment. More resources will shift the PPF to the right. However, fewer consumption goods will be produced so economic growth comes by sacrificing current consumption for investment in capital goods for future use.

PROBLEMS

1. Middleburg has the following PPF illustrating efficient combinations of food and clothing:

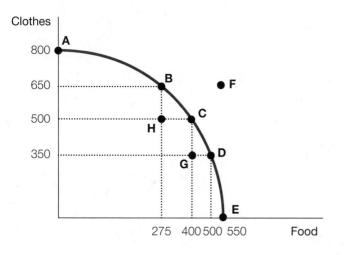

a) Calculate the opportunity costs going:

From A to B:

From B to C:

From C to D:

From D to C:

From G to D:

From G to H:

From G to C:

b) What are two possible ways Middleburg could consume at point F?

2. Carolyn and Jen each run a food cart that sells pretzels and hot dogs. Carolyn can produce and sell 720 pretzels or 320 hotdogs in an 8-hour shift. Jen lives in a different city and can only sell for a 6-hour shift, but in that time she can produce and sell 480 pretzels or 250 hot dogs.

   a) Calculate the opportunity costs of each food item for both Carolyn and Jen.

b) Does anyone have a comparative advantage in either food? Why or why not?

c) Calculate the productivity of Carolyn and Jen for both goods.

d) Does anyone have an absolute advantage in the production of either good? Why or why not?

e) Suppose Carolyn and Jen decide to merge, becoming one large vendor in Carolyn's town. How should they divide the cooking of the pretzels and hotdogs between them? Why?

3. Junior and Danica live on adjacent farms in a very rural, virtually uninhabited part of the prairies. They each grow fruit and vegetables, and each consumes exactly what each produces. They don't know each other and fend for themselves. Here are their PPFs:

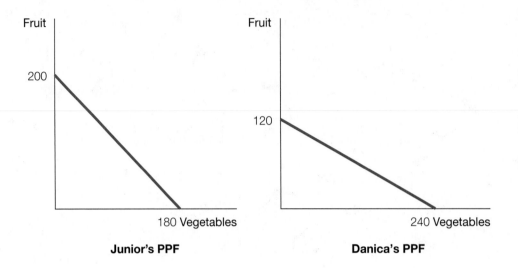

Junior's PPF   **Danica's PPF**

a) What are Junior and Danica's opportunity costs of producing both foodstuffs?

b) Suppose Junior produces and consumes 100 fruit and 90 vegetables. Danica produces and consumes 60 fruit and 120 vegetables. Indicate these consumption combinations on the PPFs above.

c) Should Junior and Danica meet up and trade with each other? Why or why not, and give details.

d) Suppose Junior and Danica do meet and decide to trade. They set a price of 1 fruit = 1.25 vegetables. Each specializes their production, and Junior trades 80 fruit to Danica in return for the appropriate number of vegetables. Fill in the table below:

	Junior		Danica	
	Fruit	**Vegetables**	**Fruit**	**Vegetables**
Without Trade				
Produce and Consume	100	90	60	120
With Trade				
Produce				
Trade	−80		+80	
Consume				
Gain				

e) On your diagram for this question, illustrate Junior and Danica's new consumption combination after trade takes place.

4. On the following diagrams, illustrate what happens to the PPF given each scenario.

   a) Immigration into the economy impacts both sectors equally.

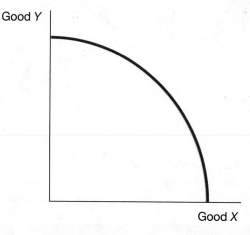

   b) A negative economic shock impacts the amount of resources used in the production of Good Y only.

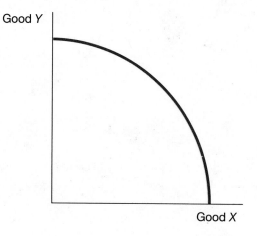

c) A new technology increases productivity in the Good X sector only.

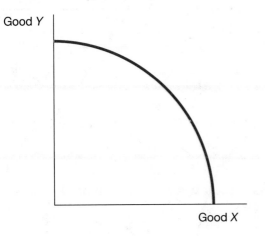

d) New early retirement laws negatively impact both sectors, but the Good X sector is hurt proportionately more than the Good Y sector.

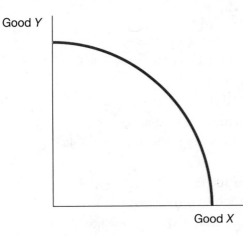

1. Middleburg has the following PPF illustrating efficient combinations of food and clothing:

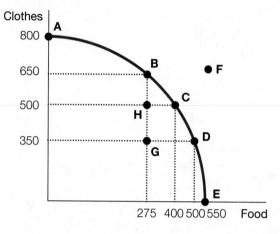

a) Calculate the opportunity costs going:

From A to B:

To get 275 food, give up 150 clothes.

To get 1 food, give up 150/275 = 0.55 clothes.

The opportunity cost of a food is 0.55 clothes going from A to B.

From B to C:

To get 125 food, give up 150 clothes.

To get 1 food, give up 150/125 = 1.2 clothes.

The opportunity cost of a food is 1.2 clothes going from B to C.

From C to D:

To get 100 food, give up 150 clothes.

To get 1 food, give up 150/100 = 1.5 clothes.

The opportunity cost of a food is 1.5 clothes going from C to D.

From D to C:

To get 150 clothes, give up 100 food.

To get 1 clothes, give up 100/150 = 0.67 food.

The opportunity cost of a clothes is 0.67 food going from D to C.

Or, shortcut: the opportunity cost of a clothes is the inverse of the opportunity cost of food = 1/1.5 = 0.67 food.

From G to D:

To get 225 food, give up 0 clothes.

To get 1 food, give up 0/225 = 0 clothes.

The opportunity cost of a food is 0 clothes, which makes sense because we aren't on the PPF so no trade-off is necessary.

From G to H:

To get 150 clothes, give up 0 food.

To get 1 clothes, give up 0/150 = 0 food.

The opportunity cost of clothing is 0 food, and again, we're not on the PPF so no trade off is necessary.

From G to C:

Again, no opportunity cost. In fact, we are getting more of both goods.

b) What are two possible ways Middleburg could consume at point F?

1. If the resource endowment increases or the technology improves, the PPF could shift over time.

2. If they trade with another economy (because comparative advantage exists) they could consume outside their PPF and enjoy gains from trade.

2. Carolyn and Jen each run a food cart that sells pretzels and hot dogs. Carolyn can produce and sell 720 pretzels or 320 hotdogs in an 8-hour shift. Jen lives in a different city and can only sell for a 6-hour shift, but in that time she can produce and sell 480 pretzels or 250 hot dogs.

a) Calculate the opportunity costs of each food item for both Carolyn and Jen.

For Carolyn:

To get 320 hot dogs, give up 720 pretzels.

To get 1 hot dog, give up 720/320 = 2.25 pretzels.

The opportunity cost of a hot dog is 2.25 pretzels.

The opportunity cost of a pretzel = 1 / 2.25 = 0.44 hot dogs.

For Jen:

To get 250 hot dogs, give up 480 pretzels.

To get 1 hot dog, give up 480/250 = 1.92 pretzels.

The opportunity cost of a hot dog is 1.92 pretzels.

The opportunity cost of a pretzel = 1 / 1.92 = 0.53 hot dogs.

b) Does anyone have a comparative advantage in either food? Why or why not?

Yes. Carolyn has a lower opportunity cost of a pretzel (0.44 hot dogs versus 0.53 hot dogs) so she has comparative advantage in the production of pretzels. Jen, therefore, has a comparative advantage in the production of hotdogs (she gives up 1.92 pretzels versus 2.25 pretzels).

c) Calculate the productivity of Carolyn and Jen for both goods.

For Carolyn: Productivity in pretzels = 720/8 = 90 pretzels per hour.

Productivity in hot dogs = 320/8 = 40 hot dogs per hour.

For Jen: Productivity in pretzels = 480/6 = 80 pretzels per hour.

Productivity in hot dogs = 250/6 = 41.7 hot dogs per hour.

d) Does anyone have an absolute advantage in the production of either good? Why or why not?

Carolyn is more productive in pretzels so she has absolute advantage in the production of pretzels.

Jen is more productive in hot dogs so she has absolute advantage in the production of hot dogs.

e) Suppose Carolyn and Jen decide to merge becoming one large vendor in Carolyn's town. How should they divide the cooking of the pretzels and hotdogs between them? Why?

Since Carolyn has the comparative advantage in pretzels, she should specialize in the production of pretzels.

Likewise, Jen has the comparative advantage in hot dogs and she should specialize in the production of hot dogs.

3. Junior and Danica live on adjacent farms in a very rural, virtually uninhabited part of the prairies. They each grow fruit and vegetables, and each consumes exactly what they produce. They don't know each other and fend for themselves. Here are their PPFs:

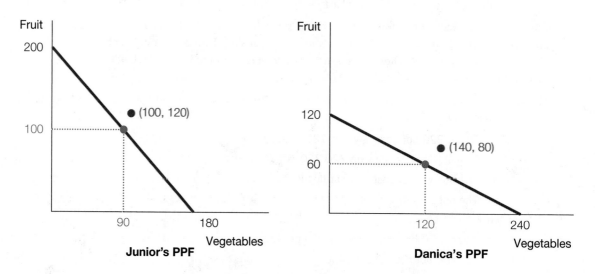

a) What are Junior and Danica's opportunity costs of producing both foodstuffs?
For Junior:

To get 200 fruit, give up 180 vegetables.

To get 1 fruit, give up 180/200 = 0.9 vegetables.

The opportunity cost of a fruit is 0.9 vegetables.

The opportunity cost of a vegetable = 1 / 0.9 = 1.1 fruit.

For Danica:

To get 120 fruit, give up 240 vegetables.

To get 1 fruit, give up 240/120 = 2 vegetables.

The opportunity cost of a fruit is 2 vegetables.

The opportunity cost of a vegetable = 1 / 2 = 0.5 fruit.

b) Suppose Junior produces and consumes 100 fruit and 90 vegetables. Danica produces and consumes 60 fruit and 120 vegetables. Indicate these consumption combinations on the PPFs above.

On diagram, in blue.

c) Should Junior and Danica meet up and trade with each other? Why or why not, and give details.

Since Junior has the comparative advantage in fruit (Junior gives up 0.9 vegetables versus 2 vegetables for Danica), he should specialize in the production of fruit and trade fruit to Danica for vegetables.

Likewise, Danica has the comparative advantage in vegetables (Danica gives up 0.5 fruit versus 1.1 fruit for Junior) and she should specialize in the production of vegetables and trade vegetables to Junior for fruit.

d) Suppose Junior and Danica do meet and decide to trade. They set a price of 1 fruit = 1.25 vegetables. Each specializes their production, and Junior trades 80 fruit to Danica in return for the appropriate number of vegetables.

Fill in the table below:

Each will specialize in the production of the good in which they have the comparative advantage. Junior produces only fruit and Danica produces only vegetables.

	Junior		Danica	
	Fruit	Vegetables	Fruit	Vegetables
Without Trade				
Produce and Consume	100	90	60	120
With Trade				
Produce	200	0	0	240
Trade	−80	100	+80	−100
Consume	120	100	80	140
Gain	+20	+10	+20	+20

e) On your diagram for this question, illustrate Junior and Danica's new consumption combination after trade takes place.

In green on the diagram. Notice that they both can now consume at a point outside their PPF.

4. On the following diagrams, illustrate what happens to the PPF given each scenario.

a) Immigration into the economy impacts both sectors equally.

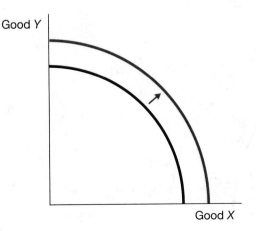

b) A negative economic shock impacts the amount of resources used in the production of Good Y only.

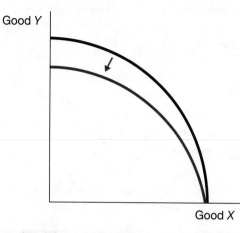

c) A new technology increases productivity in the Good X sector only.

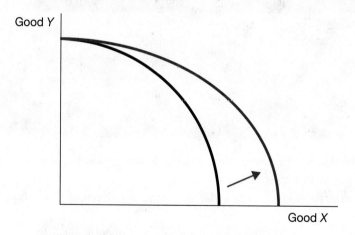

d) New early retirement laws negatively impact both sectors, but the Good X sector is hurt proportionately more than the Good Y sector.

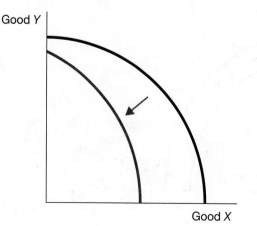

CHAPTER 3
Demand, Supply, Equilibrium

MAIN CONCEPTS AND DEFINITIONS

Market: a group of buyers and sellers of a good or service. It doesn't have to be a physical place like a fruit market where they meet face to face—think of Amazon.com as an example.

There are different structures of markets. Let's limit ourselves to working with just one for the next while. We'll investigate the market structure often considered to be the "ideal" when it comes to efficiency and maximizing peoples' economic well-being:

Perfect competition (*competition* for short):

- Many buyers and sellers act independently from each other.

- Firms produce identical (homogeneous) products.

- Firms can enter or exit the market freely. There are no barriers to entry and nothing can force a firm to stay in an industry. Resources are perfectly mobile (they can move seamlessly from one industry to another).

- Because there are so many buyers and sellers, no single individual or firm can influence the market (they're like a drop in an ocean). That means no one can affect the price at which a good sells. In perfect competition, consumers and firms are **price takers**: Buyers know the price they have to pay and sellers know the price they will receive; they take the going price as given.

What is the price? Where does it come from? It comes from the <u>entire</u> market. All the consumers who want to buy a good or service together constitute market demand. All the firms who want to produce and sell a good or service together constitute market supply. When market demand meets up with market supply, a **market price** will be established that makes buyers and sellers the best-off they can be. We'll see how this works soon.

ALERT: Let's just call goods and services "goods" for short. We know services are included.

DEMAND

Quantity demanded, Q_d, is the amount of a good consumers (buyers) are willing and able to buy at a given price, P.

Law of Demand: As P increases, Q_d decreases and vice versa. The higher the price, the less consumers are willing or able to buy of a good. We say P and Q_d have a negative relationship—they move in opposite directions.

EXAMPLE: DEMAND FOR CANDY BARS

Consider the demand for candy bars. For simplicity, assume there are only 2 consumers in the candy-bar market, Kylie and Jack. They each were asked how many candy bars they were willing and able to buy at various prices; that's how we got their individual demand. We asked them to forget about the other things that could affect how much they wanted to buy and just isolate the impact of price. To get the entire market demand, add up the quantities of each of their demands at every price:

Price	Kylie's Q_d	Jack's Q_d	Market Q
$0.50	10	15	25
$1.00	8	12	20
$1.50	6	9	15
$2.00	4	6	10
$2.50	2	3	5
$3.00	0	0	0

Let's plot these combinations of P and market Q. Q always goes on the horizontal axis.

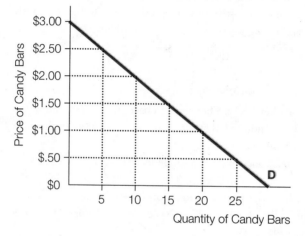

Notice the Law of Demand in action. As P goes up, Q_d goes down. When the price of the good changes, the Q_d of the good changes. This is called a **change in quantity demanded**. We move up and down a demand curve as price changes to see the corresponding quantity demanded. The demand curve DOES NOT MOVE—it stays where it is.

A Change in Quantity Demanded

- movement along a demand curve when the price of the good changes

- the demand curve itself does NOT move

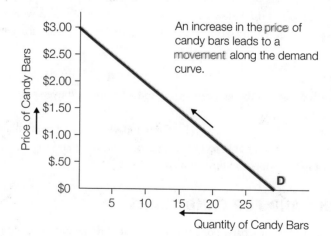

An increase in the price of candy bars leads to a movement along the demand curve.

So, price affects quantity demanded. What else affects demand?

Determinants of demand other than the price of the good

When things other than the price of the good itself changes, the entire demand curve is affected—it will shift (move) from its original position. A change in demand is a **shift of the demand curve**.

If something increases demand, the demand curve will shift out to the right.

If something decreases demand, the demand curve will shift in to the left.

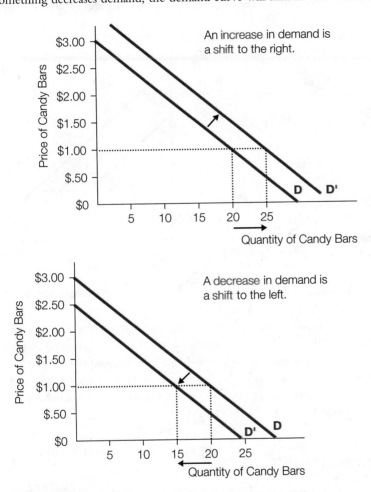

A Change in Demand

- a shift in the demand curve when something other than the price of the good changes

- the demand curve itself MOVES

What will shift the demand curve? Changes to any of the following:

Income: The higher a consumer's income, the more that consumer can buy of a good at any price. Usually, the demand curve shifts right if the consumer's demand is higher (and vice versa); however, this depends on what kind of good it is:

- **Normal Good**: If income rises, you demand more of the good. Most goods are normal.
- **Inferior Good**: If income rises, you demand less of the good. Think of it as a good you don't like but that you buy because you can't afford anything else. When income rises, you can afford something you like better so you demand less of the inferior good.

Prices of Related Consumption Goods: Goods can be substitutes for each other, they can complement each other, or they can have no relationship to each other at all.

- **Substitutes** are goods that could replace each other because they are so close to each other in characteristics. Consider printer paper. If you're not that environmentally conscious, either regular or recycled paper will do the job. If recycled paper prices rise, the quantity demanded for recycled paper will go down and the demand for regular paper will increase. We have a decrease in quantity demanded for recycled paper (P goes up, Q_d goes down) and an increase in demand for regular paper (the entire demand curve for regular paper shifts right). It would look like this:

An increase in the price of recycled paper decreases the Q_d of recycled paper and increases the demand for regular paper.

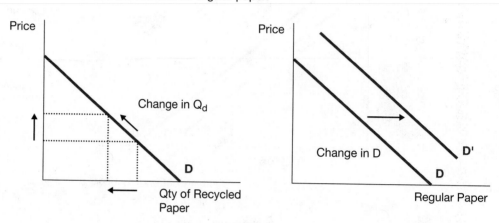

Decrease in Qty Demanded of Recycled Paper   Increase in Demand for Regular Paper

- **Complements** are goods that you tend to use together. Consider printers and ink cartridges. If the price of printers goes up, the quantity demanded of printers will decrease. If fewer printers are sold, the demand for ink for printers will decrease. We have a decrease in quantity demanded of printers (P goes up, Q_d goes down) and a decrease in demand for ink (the entire demand curve for ink cartridges shifts left). It would look like this:

An increase in the price of printers decreases the Q_d of printers and decreases the demand for ink cartridges.

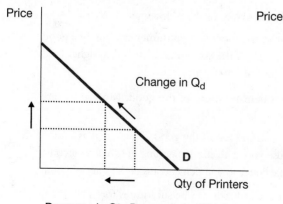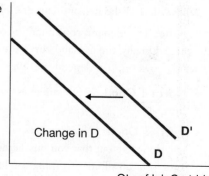

Decrease in Qty Demanded of Printers   Decrease in Demand for Ink Cartridges

Consumer Expectations: If you think the price of a good you like is going to increase in the <u>future</u>, your demand for that good will increase <u>today</u> and the demand curve for <u>today</u> will shift right (and vice versa). Don't mix this up with a change in current price, which leads to movement along the demand curve (a change in quantity demanded); a change in expectations will lead to a change in demand and a <u>shift</u> of the demand curve.

Tastes: If something (like advertising, for example) steers consumers' preferences toward a good, there will be more buyers for that good, demand for that good will increase, and the demand curve will shift right (and vice versa).

Population: More people means more consumers which means more demand at any price, so an increase in population will increase demand and shift the demand curve to the right (and vice versa). Any change in the number of buyers will shift the demand curve accordingly.

SUPPLY

Quantity supplied, Q_s, is the amount of a good producers (or firms, or sellers) are willing and able to produce and sell at a given price, P.

Law of Supply: As P increases, Q_s increases and vice versa. Focusing only on price, the higher the price, the more profitable selling the good becomes and the more of a good producers are willing and able to supply. We say P and Q_s have a positive relationship—they move together in the same direction.

EXAMPLE: SUPPLY OF CANDY BARS

Suppose, for simplicity, that there are only 2 suppliers producing candy bars, Paul and John. They were asked how many candy bars they were willing and able to supply at various prices to determine their individual supplies. Just as we did for our consumers, we asked our sellers to isolate the impact of price on how much they would supply and ignore any other things that could affect their supply. We added their individual quantities supplied at each price to get the market supply.

Price	Paul's Q_s	John's Q_s	Market Q
$0.50	2	3	5
$1.00	5	5	10
$1.50	7	8	15
$2.00	9	12	20
$2.50	11	14	25
$3.00	13	17	30

This is a **supply** <u>schedule</u>. It shows a clear relationship between price and quantity supplied.

Let's plot these P and Q$_s$ combinations:

This is a **supply curve**. It's a graph of a supply schedule. It also shows a clear relationship between price and quantity supplied.

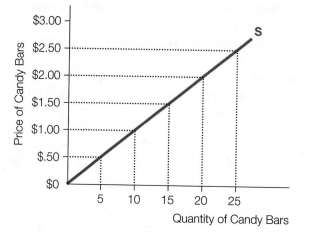

Notice that as P increases, Q increases. This is the Law of Supply at work. When the price of the good changes, the Q$_s$ of the good changes. This is called a **change in quantity supplied**. We move up and down a supply curve as price changes to see the corresponding quantity supplied. The supply curve DOES NOT MOVE. It stays where it is.

A Change in Quantity Supplied

- movement along a supply curve when the price of the good changes

- the supply curve itself does NOT move

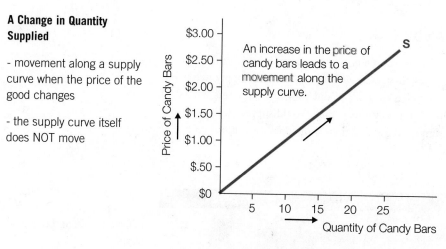

An increase in the price of candy bars leads to a movement along the supply curve.

Determinants of supply other than the selling price of the good

When things other than the price of the good itself changes, the entire supply curve is affected. It will shift (move) from its original position. A change in supply is a **shift of the supply curve**.

If something increases supply, the supply curve will shift to the right.

If something decreases supply, the supply curve will shift to the left.

A Change in Supply

- a shift in the supply curve
when something other
than the price of the good
changes

- the supply curve itself
MOVES

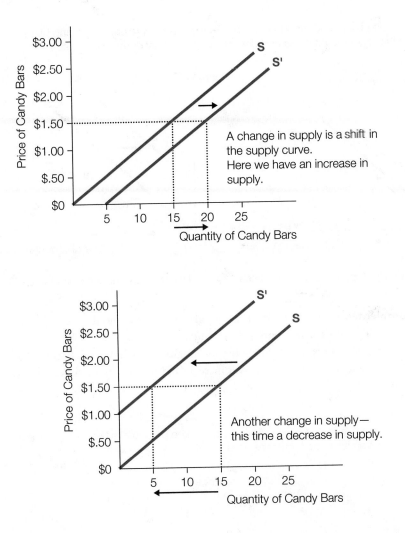

A change in supply is a shift in
the supply curve.
Here we have an increase in
supply.

Another change in supply—
this time a decrease in supply.

What factors will make the supply curve shift?

Input Prices: When the price of an input into production (a factor of production like labour, raw materials, machinery, energy, and so on)—increases, producing the good becomes less profitable and firms will offer fewer goods for sale at any price. The supply curve will shift left (and vice versa).

Prices of Related Goods in Production: Goods can be substitutes in production, complements in production, or not related at all.

- **Substitutes in production** are goods where if the selling price of one good increases, the quantity supplied of that good will increase (more profitable to produce) and the supply of the other (substitute) good will decrease. Consider a firm that produces both racing bicycles and mountain bicycles. If the selling price of racing bikes increases, the firm will want to produce and sell more racing bikes and consequently produce fewer mountain bikes. The quantity supplied of racing bikes will increase due to the price increase and the supply of mountain bikes will decrease.

Consider racing bikes and mountain bikes. An increase in the price of racing bikes increases the Q$_s$ of racing bikes and decreases the supply of mountain bikes.

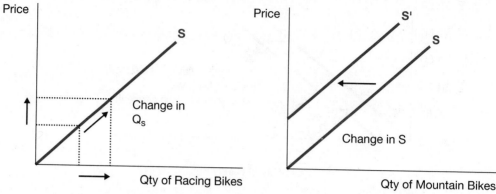

Increase in Qty Supplied of Racing Bikes   Decrease in Supply of Mountain Bikes

- **Complements in production** are goods that are produced together. Consider chicken legs and chicken wings. If a plant is producing chicken legs, they're also producing chicken wings (and breasts and thighs). If the price of chicken legs goes up, the quantity supplied of legs will increase and the supply of chicken wings will increase.

Consider chicken legs and wings. An increase in the price of chicken legs increases the Q$_s$ of chicken legs and increases the supply of chicken wings.

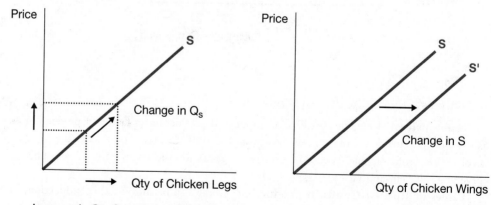

Increase in Qty Supplied of Chicken Legs   Increase in Supply of Chicken Wings

Technological Advancements: Advancements that ultimately make an item cheaper to produce will increase supply and shift the curve to the right.

Producer Expectations: What sellers expect market conditions to be in the future can affect their supply of a good today. Current supply could increase or decrease depending on the sellers' reactions to expected changes.

Number of Firms: More firms means more is produced overall, so an increase in the number of sellers will increase supply and shift the curve to the right (and vice versa).

THE MARKET: DEMAND MEETS SUPPLY

We mentioned earlier that when market demand meets market supply, market price is established. Here's how it works.

Equilibrium is a situation in which there is no incentive for anyone individually to change what they're doing because they can't make themselves any better off.

In the market, equilibrium means that consumers are buying all the goods that they want to buy at the going price and producers are selling all the goods that they want to sell at the going price. There are no goods that remain unsold (no surpluses) and no one who wants to buy at the going price goes without (no shortages). The **market clears**. This happens when the quantity demanded equals the quantity supplied.

The **market is in equilibrium when $Q_d = Q_s$**. The price where this happens is **equilibrium price** and the quantity actually sold at that price is the **equilibrium quantity traded**.

To find equilibrium using demand and supply schedules, look for a price where $Q_d = Q_s$. In our candy bar market, that happens at an equilibrium price of $1.50. The equilibrium quantity traded is 15 candy bars.

Price	Market Q_d	Price	Market Q_s
$0.50	25	$0.50	5
$1.00	20	$1.00	10
$1.50	15	$1.50	15
$2.00	10	$2.00	20
$2.50	5	$2.50	25
$3.00	0	$3.00	30

On a diagram, equilibrium occurs where the demand curve and supply curve intersect:

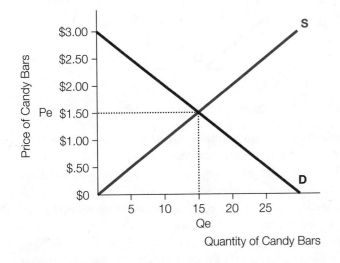

MARKETS NOT IN EQUILIBRIUM

If the price, for whatever reason, is below equilibrium, there will be excess demand—a **shortage**—in the market. Q_d will exceed Q_s at such a low price.

Example: P < Pe

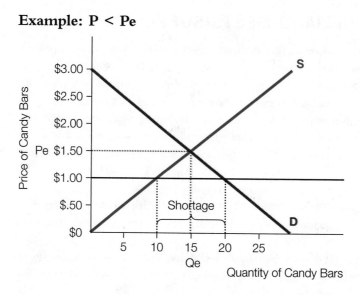

If the price is above equilibrium price, there will be excess supply—a **surplus**—in the market. Q_s will exceed Q_d at such a high price.

Example: P < Pe

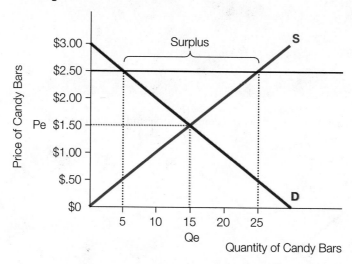

Whenever $Q_d \neq Q_s$, the lesser of the two quantities will be the quantity that actually gets traded. We say the **short side of the market** dominates. If there is a shortage where $Q_s < Q_d$, the amount Q_s will be the amount sold. Consumers can only buy what is actually produced and available for sale. If there is a surplus where $Q_d < Q_s$, the amount Q_d will be the amount sold. Producers will only be able to sell what consumers are willing to buy.

In a **free market** where buyers and sellers are able to interact without any interference or intervention (by a government, for example), the market will always return to equilibrium. As long as price is allowed to adjust (not frozen at an artificial amount), market forces will lead buyers and sellers to adjust their demand and supply until price returns to equilibrium price and the quantity traded returns to equilibrium quantity. In the case of a surplus, sellers will unload their excess inventory by lowering prices; consumers will buy more and eventually price will fall back to equilibrium price with no more surplus. In the case of a shortage, consumers will bid up the price; sellers will supply more and eventually price will rise back up to equilibrium price with no more shortage.

CHANGES IN EQUILIBRIUM

Whenever a demand curve, supply curve, or both shift as a result of a change in something other than the price of the good, there will be a new intersection of demand and supply and therefore a new equilibrium.

REMINDER: A change in price will not shift either the demand or supply curve. If price is any price but equilibrium, you'll have either a shortage or surplus, but the curves stay where they are. If something changes in any non-price determinant of demand or supply, then the affected curve will shift.

There also could be an **economic shock**—something that happens outside of a market but has an economic impact in the market nonetheless. A shock shifts either or both curves. For example, suppose a tornado destroys thousands of acres of prairie wheat. The tornado is a negative shock that reduces the wheat supply, leading to less bread and less cereal and higher prices for both.

EXAMPLE: AN INCREASE IN DEMAND

At Halloween, the demand for candy bars increases at every price because households want goodies for trick-or-treaters. The demand curve shifts to the right. At the intersection of the new demand curve and the supply curve, price has increased and quantity traded has increased, compared to the initial equilibrium.

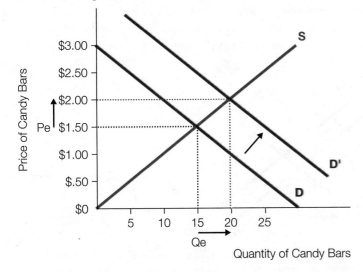

EXAMPLE: A DECREASE IN SUPPLY

Suppose a major typhoon has wiped out the majority of sugar cane fields in Southeast Asia (this is a negative economic shock). The supply of sugar decreases, resulting in an increased price of sugar, a very important ingredient in candy bars. The increase in the cost of candy-bar production leads to a decrease in the supply of candy bars at any price and the supply of candy bars shifts left. At the intersection of the new supply curve and the demand curve, price has increased and quantity traded has decreased compared to the original equilibrium.

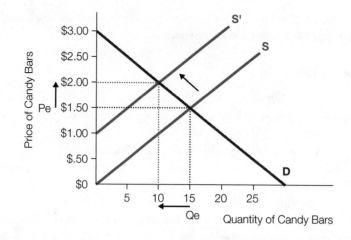

If both curves shift, what happens to equilibrium price and quantity will depend on the relative magnitude of the shifts. Which was bigger—the shift of the demand curve or the shift of the supply curve? Let's find out.

EXAMPLE: A SIMULTANEOUS INCREASE IN DEMAND AND DECREASE IN SUPPLY

Suppose Halloween and the typhoon combine to shift both curves as they did above. Now suppose that the decrease in supply was relatively larger in magnitude compared to the increase in demand. In this case, equilibrium price goes up and equilibrium quantity decreases.

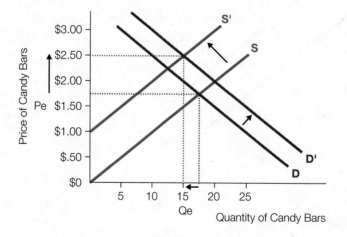

Now, instead, suppose that the increase in demand was relatively larger in magnitude compared to the decrease in supply. In this case, equilibrium price goes up again, but this time equilibrium quantity increases.

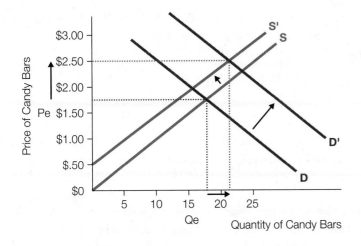

When we can't be sure how equilibrium price or quantity changes without knowing the relative magnitudes of the demand and supply curve shifts, we say that the change in price or quantity is **ambiguous**. In our example, we would say that if demand increases and supply decreases, equilibrium price will rise but the change in equilibrium quantity will be ambiguous.

Here's a summary of how equilibrium price and quantity change when curves shift:

	No Change in Demand	An Increase in Demand	A Decrease in Demand
No Change in Supply	P Q	P rises Q rises	P falls Q falls
An Increase in Supply	P falls Q rises	P ambiguous Q rises	P falls Q ambiguous
A Decrease in Supply	P rises Q falls	P rises Q ambiguous	P ambiguous Q falls

THE ALGEBRA OF DEMAND AND SUPPLY

WHY DEMAND AND SUPPLY CURVES SHIFT

To oversimplify, anything that affects the P-intercept will shift demand or supply. So, where does that P-intercept come from?

Q_d is a function of the price of the good, consumer income, prices of related goods, expectations, population, and tastes. For this example, let's just consider three of those determinants (we can also call determinants **variables**, because the values they take can vary). Let's include the price of the good, consumer income, and prices of related goods as determinants of demand (these probably are the most interesting to economists, as we'll see in the next chapter).

Consider the regional market for housing. Demand for single detached homes depends on the price of the house, P_H; consumer income, N (N is the traditional letter for income); and the price of related goods, say, townhouses, P_T. Suppose an economist studies the market and determines an equation that accurately depicts the impacts of these three variables on Q_d:

$$Q_d = 0.2N + 0.05P_T - 11\ 400P_H.$$

Suppose that average consumer income is N = $50 000 and the average price of town-houses is $285 000. Let's substitute these values into our equation:

$$Q_d = 0.2N + 0.05P_T - 0.01P_H$$

$$Q_d = 0.2(50\ 000) + 0.05(285\ 000) - 0.01P_H$$

$$Q_d = 10\ 000 + 14\ 250 - 0.01P_H$$

$$Q_d = 24\ 250 - 0.01P_H$$

This is a linear demand curve typical of the ones we'll be working with shortly. And look at our equation—we have an intercept. That value of 24 250 represents the "snapshot" value of consumer income and the price of a related good. If either consumer income or the price of townhouses changes, the value of the intercept will change and our demand curve will shift. Notice that in the first equation, there is a positive sign on the price of townhouses variable. That's because townhouses and single detached homes are substitutes. If the price of townhouses increases, the Q_d of single detached homes will increase. The negative sign on the P_H variable tells us that as the price of single detached homes increases, Q_d decreases, as we would expect.

If the average price of single detached houses is $375 000, the demand for single detached houses will be $Q_d = 24\ 250 - 0.01(375\ 000) = 20\ 500$ houses. If the average price of single detached homes increases to $425 000, $Q_d = 24\ 250 - 0.01(425\ 000) = 20\ 000$. As P_H increases, the Q_d of single detached homes decreases. We didn't let consumer income or the price of the related townhouses change; we kept them constant—we kept other things equal. That's why earlier we asked Kylie and Jack to isolate the impact of price on their demand for candy bars and forget about other determinants which remain constant.

The same concepts hold for the supply curve. Q_s is a function of the price of the good and other determinants (variables): production costs, prices of related goods in production, number of firms, technology, and expectations. Our same economist estimated an equation that depicts the impact of the price of single detached homes, P_H; production costs, C; and selling prices of a related good in production, say, townhouses, P_T; on Q_s:

$$Q_s = 0.7P_H - 0.3C - 0.6P_T$$

Suppose that the average cost of a single detached house is $295 000 and the average selling price of a townhouse is $249 000. Let's substitute these values into our equation:

$$Q_s = 0.7P_H - 0.3(295\ 000) - 0.6(249\ 000)$$

$$Q_s = 0.7P_H - 88\ 500 - 149\ 400$$

$$Q_s = 0.7P_H - 237\ 900$$

This is a typical linear supply curve with a—you guessed it—intercept. The value of 237 900 is the "snapshot" value of production cost and townhouse prices, and if either changes, the intercept changes and the supply curve shifts. Looking at the first equation, the negative sign on production costs, C, tells us that as costs increase, the Q_s of single detached homes will decrease. Likewise, the negative sign on P_T tells us that as townhouse prices increase, builders will want to build and sell more townhouses so the supply of single detached homes will decrease. And the positive sign on the P_H variable indicates that as the price of single detached homes rises, Q_s also rises.

If the average price of single detached houses is $375 000, the supply of single detached houses will be $Q_s = 0.7(375\ 000) - 237\ 900 = 24\ 600$ houses. If the average price of single detached homes increases to $425 000, $Q_s = 0.7(425\ 000) - 237\ 900 = 59\ 600$.

As P_H increases, the Q_s of single detached homes increases. We didn't let costs or the price of the related townhouses change; we again kept them constant. That's why earlier we asked Paul and John to isolate the impact of price on their supply of candy bars and forget about other determinants which remain constant.

KEY TERMS

market

perfect competition

price taker

market price

quantity demanded, Q_d

Law of Demand

demand schedule

demand curve

change in quantity demanded

shift of the demand curve

income

normal good

inferior good

prices of related consumption goods

substitutes

complements

consumer expectations

tastes

population/changes in the number of buyers

quantity supplied, Q_s

Law of Supply

supply schedule

supply curve

change in quantity supplied

shift of the supply curve

input prices

prices of related goods in production

substitutes in production

complements in production

technological advancements

producer expectations

number of firms

equilibrium

market clears

market is in equilibrium when $Q_d = Q_s$

equilibrium price

equilibrium quantity traded

shortage

surplus

short side of the market

free market

economic shock

ambiguous

variables

SOLVED EXAMPLE PROBLEMS

As we have seen in this chapter, the competitive market is in equilibrium when supply and demand are equal. Since we have assumed, for simplicity, that supply and demand are linear functions, we can use basic algebra to solve for equilibrium price and quantity traded. We just saw what demand and supply equations for houses might look like and economists often do estimate these equations for different industries. So, it is not a giant leap for us to use equations, too.

EXAMPLE 1

Suppose we are told that in the market for USB flash drives, demand is given by $Q_d = 100 - 3P$ and supply is given by $Q_s = 2P + 20$.

First of all, notice that the coefficient on price in the demand equation is negative. It should be, since we know the demand curve is negatively sloped. Similarly, the coefficient on price in the supply curve is positive, since the supply curve is positively sloped.

Second, notice that both equations are written in the form Q = f(P). But when we graph supply and demand, P is on the y axis. What we actually graph are the inverse demand and inverse supply curves. We can derive these inverse equations simply by rewriting them so that P is on the left-hand side.

For the inverse demand equation:

$$Q_d = 100 - 3P$$
$$3P = 100 - Q_d$$
$$P = 100/3 - Q_d/3 \qquad \text{(notice the curve is still negatively sloped)}$$

For the inverse supply equation:

$$Q_s = 2P + 20$$
$$2P = Q_s - 20$$
$$P = Q_s/2 - 10 \qquad \text{(notice the curve is still positively sloped)}$$

We can solve for equilibrium using either set of equations. The only difference is that if we use the Q = equations, we find equilibrium P first and then equilibrium quantity traded; if we use the inverse P = equations, we find equilibrium quantity traded first and then equilibrium P.

Now, let's solve the original equations to find equilibrium P and Q:

In equilibrium, $Q_d = Q_s$ (note that this is true only in equilibrium). Set $Q_d = Q_s$:

$$100 - 3P = 2P + 20$$
$$80 = 5P$$
$$P = 16 \text{ so equilibrium price is \$16.}$$

Now substitute P = 16 into either the demand or supply equation to get equilibrium Q. It doesn't matter which equation you pick because we set $Q_d = Q_s$ so we'll get the same quantity either way.

If we substitute P = 16 into the demand equation:

$$Q_d = 100 - 3(16)$$
$$Q_d = 52$$

If we substitute P = 16 into the supply equation:

$$Q_s = 2(16) + 20$$
$$Q_s = 52$$

Since $Q_d = Q_s$ is quantity traded in equilibrium, then equilibrium Q is 52 units of output, in this example 52 USB drives.

EXAMPLE 2

Let's use the same equations we used in the previous example.

Suppose that the market is not in equilibrium (we'll see more about this in Chapter 6). Suppose the current price in the market is \$12. What is the quantity traded in the market?

At a price of \$12, we need to calculate Q_d and Q_s separately because they will not be equal because the market is not in equilibrium. To do this, we just substitute P = 12 into both equations:

For quantity demanded:

$$Q_d = 100 - 3(12)$$
$$Q_d = 64$$

For quantity supplied:

$$Q_s = 2(12) + 20$$
$$Q_s = 44$$

Here, $Q_d > Q_s$ resulting in a shortage.

What quantity will actually be traded in the market? Our rule is that the short side dominates, so whichever is less, Q_d or Q_s, will be the amount traded. In our example, the quantity traded will be 44.

EXAMPLE 3

A huge forest fire destroys acres of spruce and fir trees meant to be cut and sold as Christmas/Holiday trees. At the same time, demand for these real trees has fallen as society has become more ecologically friendly. On the axes below, sketch the original equilibrium and then add the new equilibrium resulting from the changes just outlined.

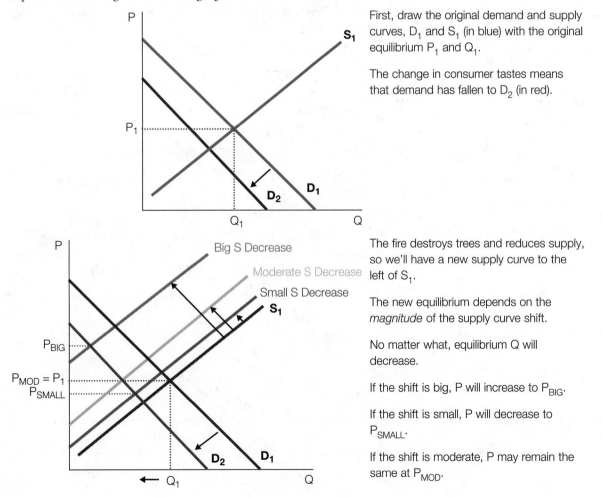

First, draw the original demand and supply curves, D_1 and S_1 (in blue) with the original equilibrium P_1 and Q_1.

The change in consumer tastes means that demand has fallen to D_2 (in red).

The fire destroys trees and reduces supply, so we'll have a new supply curve to the left of S_1.

The new equilibrium depends on the *magnitude* of the supply curve shift.

No matter what, equilibrium Q will decrease.

If the shift is big, P will increase to P_{BIG}.

If the shift is small, P will decrease to P_{SMALL}.

If the shift is moderate, P may remain the same at P_{MOD}.

EXAMPLE 4

The market demand for smartphone hard cases is given by $Q_d = 0.01N - 0.4P_{SP} - 2P_C$. P_C is the price of smartphone hard cases, N is consumer income and P_{SP} is the price of smartphones.

Suppose that average consumer income is currently $50 000 and the average price of smartphones is $300.

a) What is the demand equation for smartphone cases?

Substitute the values given for income and the price of smartphones into the equation:

$$Q_d = 0.01(50\ 000) - 0.4(300) - 2P_C$$

$$Q_d = 380 - 2P_C$$

b) How are smartphone cases and smartphones related?

The coefficient P_{SP} is negative. As the price of smartphones increases, the demand for smartphone cases decreases. Smartphones and cases are complements. This makes sense since you don't need a case if you don't have a phone; the two would be used together.

c) The supply of smartphone cases is given by $Q_s = 2P_C - 0.25C + 0.05F$. P_C is the price of smartphone cases, C is the costs of production, and F is the number of firms producing cases.

Suppose average costs are $4 and there are currently 20 firms in the industry. What is the supply equation for smartphone cases?

Substitute the values for costs and number of firms into the equation:

$$Q_s = 2P_C - 0.25(4) + 0.05(20)$$

$$Q_s = 2P_C$$

d) Using the demand and supply curves you derived above, what is the market equilibrium price and quantity?

In equilibrium, $Q_d = Q_s$ so set demand equal to supply:

$$380 - 2P_C = 2P_C$$

$$380 = 4P_C$$

$$P_C = 95$$

Set $P_C = 95$ in either the demand or supply equation (remember, it doesn't matter which one because they are set equal to each other … I'll use the supply equation).

$$Q_s = 2(95) = 190 \text{ smartphone cases}$$

So, equilibrium price and quantity are P = $95 and Q = 190 smartphone cases

e) Sketch the equilibrium from part d.

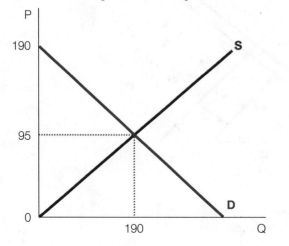

1. Demand and supply in the market for fresh, bunched carrots are given by $Q_d = 528 - 500P$ and $Q_s = 300P$. P is the price per kilogram and Q is measured in kilograms.

   a) What are equilibrium P and Q in the carrot market?

   b) If the price of carrots happened to be $1 per kilogram, what would be the quantity traded on the market? Illustrate this on the axes below (you'll need to sketch the original market equilibrium to use as a benchmark for comparison). Calculate and label the P and Q intercepts for the demand curve.

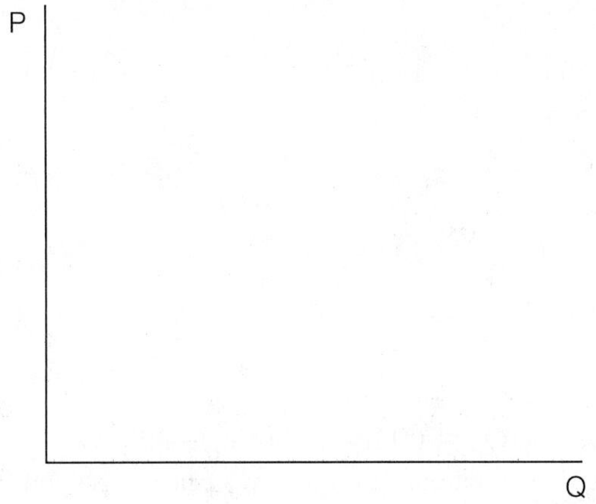

   P
   |
   |
   |
   |
   |
   |
   |
   |_____ Q

   c) Suppose the production costs of *bags* of carrots (substitutes for fresh bunches) decreases. On the axes below, illustrate what happens in the market for bags of carrots and the market for bunched carrots.

   Market for Bags of Carrots   Market for Bunches of Carrots

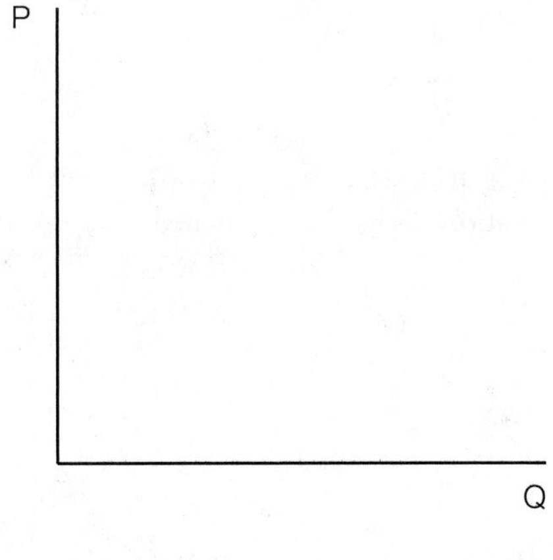

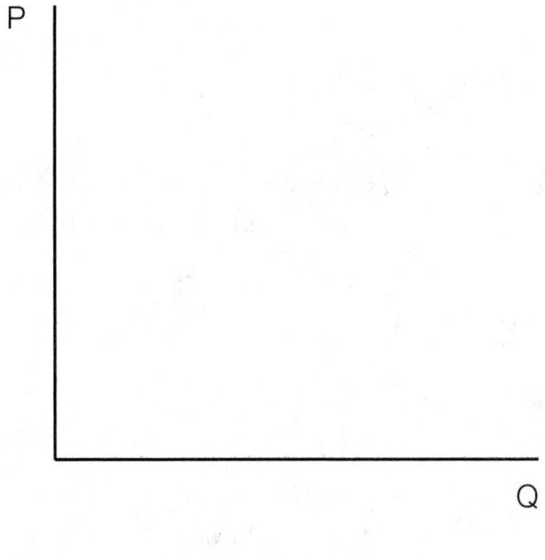

   P   P
   | |
   | |
   | |
   | |
   | |
   | |
   |_____ Q |_____ Q

2. For each of the following sets of demand and supply equations, find equilibrium P and Q.

    a) $Q_d = 60 - P$ and $Q_s = 5P$

    b) $Q_d = 90 - 4P$ and $Q_s = 10 + P$

    c) $Q_d = 4500 - 0.75P$ and $Q_s = 1000 + 3.25P$

3. Demand for gasoline today is given by $Q_d = 0.12N + 2000P_E - 3P_G$. N is average consumer income, P_E is consumers' expectations of tomorrow's price of gas and P_G is the current price of a litre of gas.

    a) What is the equation for demand when income is $60 000 and the expected price is $1.25 per litre?

    b) Suppose there is a news report that gas prices are going up to $1.50 per litre at midnight. What is the new demand equation? What has happened to the demand curve?

4. Consider equilibrium in the **market for beef steaks**. What impact would each of the following have on demand for or supply of **beef steaks** or both? In other words, how would either or both curves *shift*? Don't confuse shifts with changes in *quantity* demanded or *quantity* supplied.

Event	Demand	Supply
Pork prices rise	increase	no change
Mad cow disease affects livestock	_____	_____
Beef *roast* prices rise	_____	_____
The Keg Steak House goes bankrupt	_____	_____
Increase in the number of beef ranchers	_____	_____
Increase in the number of vegetarians	_____	_____
Cattle feed prices rise	_____	_____
Potato prices rise	_____	_____
It was a cold, wet summer in Ontario	_____	_____

SOLUTIONS

1. Demand and supply in the market for fresh, bunched carrots are given by $Q_d = 528 - 500P$ and $Q_s = 300P$. P is the price per kilogram and Q is measured in kilograms.

   a) What are equilibrium P and Q in the carrot market?

   In equilibrium, $Q_d = Q_s$

   $528 - 500P = 300P$

   $800P = 528$

   $P = \$0.66$ Substitute this into either Q_d or Q_s equation:

   $Q_s = 300(0.66) = 198$ kg

   b) If the price of bunches of carrots happened to be $1 per kilogram, what would be the quantity traded on the market? Illustrate this on the axes below (you'll need to sketch the original market equilibrium to use as a benchmark for comparison). Calculate and label the P and Q intercepts for the demand curve.

To get P-intercept, set $Q_d = 0$

$0 = 528 - 500P$

$500P = 528$

$P = \$1.06$

To get Q-intercept, set $P = 0$

$Q_d = 528 - 500(0)$

$Q_d = 528$

At $P = 1.00$:

$Q_d = 528 - 500(1) = 28$

$Q_s = 300(1) = 300$

The short side dominates so the quantity traded is 28 kg.

There is a surplus of $300 - 28 = 272$ kg.

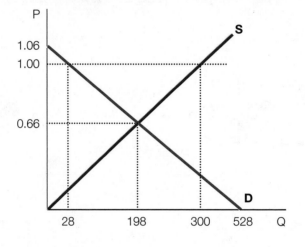

   c) Suppose the production costs of *bags* of carrots (substitutes for fresh bunches) decreases. On the axes below, illustrate what happens in the market for bags of carrots and the market for bunched carrots.

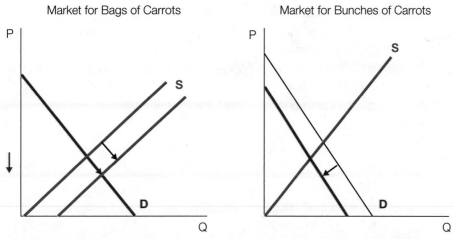

Market for Bags of Carrots   Market for Bunches of Carrots

The decrease in the production costs of bagged carrots leads to an increase (shift) in supply of bagged carrots. This leads to a decrease in the price of bags of carrots. Bagged carrots are a substitute for bunched carrots; the decrease in bagged carrots price means consumers will want to buy more bagged carrots (an increase in quantity demanded) and demand fewer bunches of carrots (a decrease in demand which shifts the demand curve for bunched carrots).

2. For each of the following sets of demand and supply equations, find equilibrium P and Q.

   a) $Q_d = 60 - P$ and $Q_s = 5P$

   In equilibrium, $Q_d = Q_s$

   $60 - P = 5P$

   $6P = 60$

   $P = \$10$ Substitute this into either Q_d or Q_s:

   $Q_s = 5(10) = 50$

   b) $Q_d = 90 - 4P$ and $Q_s = 10 + P$

   In equilibrium, $Q_d = Q_s$

   $90 - 4P = 10 + P$

   $5P = 80$

   $P = \$16$ Substitute this into either Q_d or Q_s:

   $Q_s = 10 + 16 = 26$

   c) $Q_d = 4500 - 0.75P$ and $Q_s = 1000 + 3.25P$

   In equilibrium, $Q_d = Q_s$

   $4500 - 0.75P = 1000 + 3.25P$

   $4P = 3500$

   $P = \$875$ Substitute this into either Q_d or Q_s:

   $Q_d = 4500 - 0.75(875) = 3843.75$

3. Demand for gasoline today is given by $Q_d = 0.12N + 2000P_E - 3P_G$. N is average consumer income, P_E is consumers' expectations of tomorrow's price of gas and P_G is the current price of a litre of gas.

   a) What is the equation for demand when income is \$60 000 and the expected price is \$1.25 per litre?

   $Q_d = 0.12(60\ 000) + 2000(1.25) - 3P_G$

   $Q_d = 9700 - 3P_G$

   b) Suppose there is a news report that gas prices are going up to \$1.50 per litre at midnight. What is the new demand equation? What has happened to the demand curve?

   $Q_d = 0.12(60\ 000) + 2000(1.50) - 3P_G$

   $Q_d = 10\ 200 - 3P_G$

   Expectations of the price increase at midnight increased the demand for gas today. The current demand curve has shifted to the right.

4. Consider equilibrium in the **market for beef steaks**. What impact would each of the following have on demand for or supply of beef **steaks** or both? In other words, how would either or both curves *shift*? Don't confuse shifts with changes in *quantity* demanded or *quantity* supplied.

Event	Demand	Supply
Pork prices rise	increase	no change
Mad cow disease affects livestock	decrease	decrease
Beef *roast* prices rise	increase	increase
The Keg Steak House goes bankrupt	decrease	no change
Increase in the number of beef ranchers	no change	increase
Increase in the number of vegetarians	decrease	no change
Cattle feed prices rise	no change	decrease
Potato prices rise	decrease	no change
It was a cold, wet summer in Ontario	decrease	no change

CHAPTER 4
Elasticity

MAIN CONCEPTS AND DEFINITIONS

Elasticity is a measure of how quantity demanded or supplied responds when one of their determinants change. Here are the most common elasticities:

- **Own-Price Elasticity of Demand, E_p:** the (percentage change in Q_d)/(percentage change in P). This measures how Q_d responds when the selling price of that good changes.

- **Income Elasticity of Demand, E_N:** the (percentage change in Q_d)/(percentage change in income, N). This measures how Q_d responds when the income of consumers of that good changes. If income elasticity is positive, the good is a normal good. If income elasticity is negative, the good is an inferior good. The plus or minus sign is important.

- **Cross-Price Elasticity of Demand, $E_{a,b}$:** the (percentage change in Q_d of one good, a)/(percentage change in the price of another related good, b). This measures how the Q_d of <u>one</u> good responds when the selling price of <u>another</u> related good changes. If cross-price elasticity is positive, the goods are substitutes. If cross-price elasticity is negative, the goods are complements. The plus or minus sign is important.

- **Price Elasticity of Supply, Es:** the (percentage change in Q_s)/(percentage change in P). This measures how Q_s responds when the selling price of that good changes. The Law of Supply means that the price elasticity of supply will always be positive.

When we divide the percentage change in Q by a percentage change in the determinant, we end up with a number. This number is our **coefficient of elasticity**. How big or how small, positive or negative—this coefficient gives us a lot of information about how a good responds to changes in its determinants. Firms and policymakers can benefit greatly from this knowledge.

The formula for elasticity is:

$$E = \frac{\%\Delta \text{ in } Q}{\%\Delta \text{ in determinant}}$$

ALERT: We know from the Law of Demand that as P rises, Q_d decreases and vice versa. This means that the own-price elasticity of demand coefficient will always be negative.

Because we know this, we can drop the minus sign for E_p and just consider the absolute value. Keep this in mind as we define types of elasticity below.

TYPES OF ELASTICITY

Regardless of which elasticity—demand or supply—we're talking about, how we describe elasticity is always the same:

Perfectly Inelastic: <u>Q has no response whatsoever</u> when a determinant changes. The curve is perfectly vertical. The percentage change in Q given a percentage change in the determinant is zero. We get a coefficient of elasticity equal to 0.

Inelastic: <u>Q responds only slightly</u> when a determinant changes. The curve is fairly steep. The percentage change in Q given a percentage change in the determinant is small; the numerator in our formula is smaller than the denominator. If we divide the percentage change in Q by the percentage change in the determinant, we get a coefficient of elasticity between 0 and 1.

Elastic: <u>Q responds a good deal</u> when a determinant changes. The curve is relatively flat. The percentage change in Q given a percentage change in the determinant is fairly big; the numerator in our formula is larger than the denominator. If we divide the percentage change in Q by the percentage change in the determinant, we get a coefficient of elasticity greater than 1.

Perfectly Elastic: Q responds so much to a change in a determinant that we can't even measure the change; we say the <u>response in Q is infinite</u>. The curve is perfectly horizontal. The percentage change in Q given a percentage change in the determinant is infinite. We get a coefficient of elasticity that approaches infinity.

What if the percentage change in Q is exactly the same as the percentage change in the determinant? The percentage change in Q divided by the percentage change in the determinant would equal 1. We call this **unit elasticity**. The coefficient of elasticity equals 1. Unit elasticity is one of those things that is mathematically possible but not necessarily something we'd see every day. Think of unit elasticity as the point that separates inelastic and elastic demand or supply.

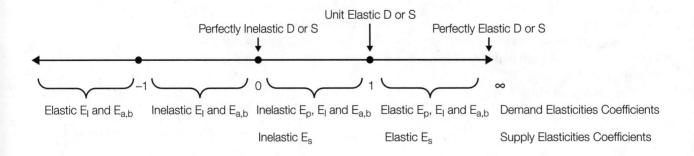

WHAT THE CURVES LOOK LIKE

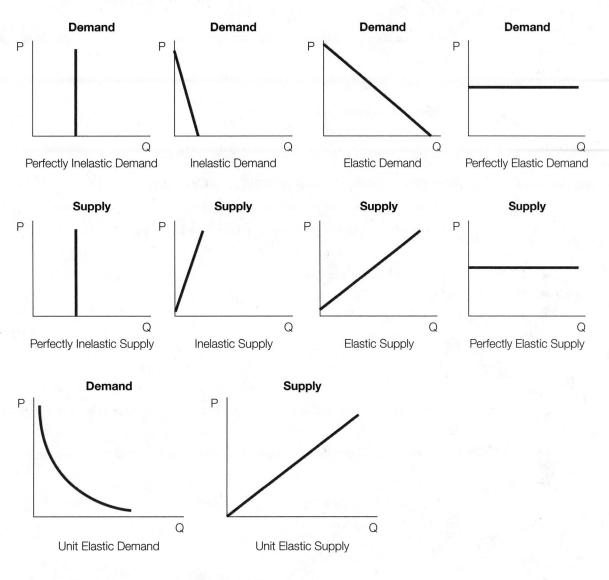

Perfectly Inelastic Demand

Inelastic Demand

Elastic Demand

Perfectly Elastic Demand

Perfectly Inelastic Supply

Inelastic Supply

Elastic Supply

Perfectly Elastic Supply

Unit Elastic Demand

Unit Elastic Supply

GENERALITIES ABOUT ELASTICITIES

What kinds of goods tend to have <u>elastic</u> demand?

- Luxury goods
- Goods that have close substitutes
- Goods for which you spend a large proportion of your budget
- Goods that are very narrowly (precisely) defined

What kinds of goods have <u>inelastic</u> demand?

- Necessities
- Goods with no close substitutes

- Goods for which you spend a small proportion of your budget
- Goods that are broadly defined

The demand for goods becomes more elastic over time.

What kinds of goods have <u>elastic</u> supply?

- Goods whose factors of production are readily available
- Goods whose factors of production are mobile
- Goods that can be easily stored
- Goods with short, non-complicated production processes

What kinds of goods have <u>inelastic</u> supply?

- Goods whose factors of production are difficult to obtain
- Goods whose factors of production are limited in mobility
- Goods that cannot be easily stored
- Goods that take a long time to produce or have a complicated production process

The supply of goods becomes more elastic over time (time is a big determinant of supply elasticity).

Can we generalize about slopes and elasticity?

- The more elastic the demand or supply, the flatter the curve.
- The more inelastic the demand or supply, the steeper the curve.
- Slope is not the same as elasticity. Slope is a rate of change; elasticity is a percentage change.

Own-price demand elasticity varies depending on where you are on a demand curve.

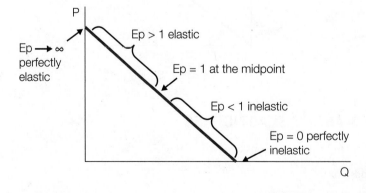

TOTAL REVENUE AND OWN-PRICE ELASTICITY OF DEMAND

If demand for a good is elastic, firms can increase total revenue TR by lowering the selling price of the good (assuming firms have the ability to set their own price).

- The lower price will attract a lot of buyers, so total sales at the end of the day actually go up (lower price but more units are sold).

If demand for a good is inelastic, firms can increase total revenue TR by increasing the selling price of the good (assuming firms have the ability to set their own price).

- The higher price will only lose a few buyers, so total sales at the end of the day actually go up (higher prices paid by the many buyers who still buy the good).

THE ALGEBRA OF ELASTICITY

Own-price elasticity of demand

$$E_p = \frac{\%\Delta \text{ in } Q_d}{\%\Delta \text{ in } P}$$

$\%\Delta$ in Q_d = [(new Q_d value − old Q_d value)/old Q_d value] $\star$ 100

$\%\Delta$ in P = [(new P value − old P value)/old P value] $\star$ 100

Since we're dividing $\frac{\%\Delta \text{ in } Q_d}{\%\Delta \text{ in } P}$, the $\star$ 100 will cancel each other out.

Note that the value of E_p depends on the direction of the price change. For example, going from \$2 and $Q_d = 5$ to \$3 and $Q_d = 3$ will give different percentage changes (and thus coefficient values) than if we calculate going from \$3 to \$2 and $Q_d = 3$ to \$2 and $Q_d = 5$. The price and quantity ranges are the same but different coefficient values will result. Let's compute it:

Going from P = \$2 and $Q_d = 5$ to P = \$3 and $Q_d = 3$:

- $\%\Delta$ in $Q_d = (3 − 5)/5 = −0.4$
- $\%\Delta$ in P $= (3 − 2)/2 = 0.5$
- $E_p = −0.4/0.5 = −0.8$ We drop the minus sign so $E_p = 0.8$, inelastic.

Going from P = \$3 and $Q_d = 3$ to P = \$2 and $Q_d = 5$:

- $\%\Delta$ in $Q_d = (5 − 3)/3 = 0.67$
- $\%\Delta$ in P $= (2 − 3)/3 = −0.33$
- $E_p = 0.67/−0.33 = −2.03$ We drop the minus sign so $E_p = 2.03$, elastic.

Be careful that you are computing the percentage change going in the right direction as needed.

Income elasticity of demand

$$E_N = \frac{\%\Delta \text{ in } Q_d}{\%\Delta \text{ in } N} \text{ where income is denoted N}$$

If $E_N > 0$, the good is a normal good.
If $E_N < 0$, the good is an inferior good.

EXAMPLE

Consumer incomes decrease from \$45 000 to \$40 000 per year. Demand for canned beans increases from 100 cans to 102 cans per year.

%Δ in Q_d = (102 − 100)/100 = 0.02

%Δ in N = (40 000 − 45 000)/45 000 = −0.11

E_N = 0.02/−0.11 = −0.18 Beans are inferior goods (E_N < 0) and income inelastic (E_N is a fraction).

Cross-price elasticity of demand

$$E_{a,b} = \frac{\%\Delta \text{ in } Q_{da}}{\%\Delta \text{ in } P_b}$$

If $E_{a,b}$ > 0, the goods are substitutes.

If $E_{a,b}$ < 0, the goods are complements.

EXAMPLE

The price of a soft drink increases from $1.99 to $2.49 per 2-litre bottle. Demand for a fruit juice increases from 500 to 1000 bottles.

%Δ in Q_d of fruit juice = (1000 − 500)/500 = 1

%Δ in P of soft drinks = (2.49 − 1.99)/1.99 = 0.25

$E_{a,b}$ = 1/0.25 = 4 Soft drinks and fruit juice are substitutes ($E_{a,b}$ > 0).

NOTE: The larger (in absolute value) the value of the cross-price elasticity coefficient, the stronger the relationship between the two goods. For example, if $E_{a,b}$ = 20.6 for one pair of goods and $E_{a,b}$ = 3.22 for another pair, the first pair are closer substitutes than the second pair. Or, if $E_{a,b}$ = −5.4 for one pair of goods and $E_{a,b}$ = −1.85 for another pair, the first pair are closer complements than the second pair. If $E_{a,b}$ = 0, the two goods are not related whatsoever.

Price elasticity of supply

$$E_s = \frac{\%\Delta \text{ in } Q_s}{\%\Delta \text{ in } P}$$

Don't forget that E_s will always be a positive number because of the Law of Supply: as P increases, Q_s increases (and vice versa).

EXAMPLE

The price of aluminum rises from $20 to $25 per tonne. Quantity supplied increases from 8 tonnes to 9 tonnes.

%Δ in Q_s = (9 − 8)/8 = 0.125

%Δ in P = (25 − 20)/20 = 0.25

E_s = 0.125/0.25 = 0.50 Supply of aluminum is price inelastic.

Point elasticity of demand

As economists, we are always concerned with the impact of marginal changes in price on quantity demanded. In other words, if price changes by just a little, how much will quantity demanded change? We can answer this question by computing the point elasticity of demand.

We know that price elasticity = percentage change in Q_d/percentage change in P. We can write this as:

$E_p = (\Delta Q/Q)/(\Delta P/P)$

Rearranging, we get $E_p = \Delta Q/\Delta P \star P/Q$

But $\Delta Q/\Delta P$ is the rate of change in Q_d with respect to price; it is the slope of the demand curve when it is written in the form $Q_d = f(P)$. So E_p = slope of the demand curve $\star$ P/Q. Technically (for those who know some calculus), $E_p = dQ/dP \star P/Q$ for any demand curve. We will get a very precise determination of elasticity using this method.

In our first-year course, all our demand curves are linear functions. This makes finding the slope easy—it is just the coefficient on P when demand is written in the form $Q_d = a - bP$.

We have seen in our diagrams that elasticity is reflected in the slope of the demand curve; the flatter the demand curve, the more price elastic is the demand. Now we know why—it's because the slope of the demand curve is part of the equation for elasticity. Here's how this works:

The slope of our linear demand curve is constant, regardless of what price and quantity level we are at. When we graph our demand curve, we are graphing the inverse demand, so whatever value we get for dQ/dP, we are actually graphing a line with slope 1/(dQ/dP) or dP/dQ.

Let's pick a point, any point, (Q, P). Now let's draw two demand curves going through the same point, one demand curve flatter than the other. P/Q is the same for both curves but the slopes are different. The bigger dQ/dP is, the more elastic is the demand curve. But a bigger dQ/dP means a smaller dP/dQ. So a bigger elasticity coefficient at (Q, P) means that we "see" a flatter demand curve when we graph it, like curve D_1. Curve D_2 is steeper, so dP/dQ is larger and therefore dQ/dP is smaller. A smaller dQ/dP means a smaller elasticity coefficient. That's why the flatter the demand curve, the more elastic is the demand curve and the steeper the demand curve, the more inelastic is the demand curve.

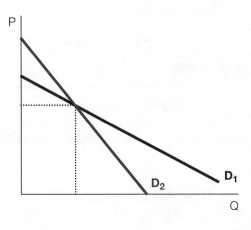

We have also seen that elasticity changes as we move up or down the demand curve. That's because for every P, there is a different corresponding Q so that P/Q is different at every point on the demand curve. Since the slope of our linear demand curve is constant, we will get a different coefficient of elasticity for every (P, Q) combination.

EXAMPLE

Demand for gadgets is given by $Q_d = 100 - 4P$.

At a price of $2, what is the point elasticity of demand?

First, we need to know what Q_d is when P = 2. Substituting P = 2 into the demand equation yields $Q_d = 92$.

The slope of our demand curve is simply −4 (the slope coefficient on P from our equation). We know that price and quantity demanded are inversely related (from our Law of Demand), so we can ignore the minus sign.

$$E_p = dQ/dP \star P/Q = 4 \star 2/92 = 0.087$$

Since 0.087 is less than 1, we know that at a price of $2, demand for gadgets is price inelastic.

What is the point elasticity of demand when price is $20?

When P = 20, $Q_d = 100 - 4(20) = 20$.

$$E_p = dQ/dP \star P/Q = 4 \star 20/20 = 4$$

Since 4 is greater than 1, we know that at a price of $20, demand for gadgets is price elastic.

Notice that at a higher price, demand is more elastic than at a lower price. This corresponds to our diagram that shows that as we move up and left along the demand curve, demand becomes more price elastic.

KEY TERMS

elasticity	perfectly inelastic
own-price elasticity of demand, E_p	inelastic
income elasticity of demand, E_N	elastic
cross-price elasticity of demand, $E_{a,b}$	perfectly elastic
price elasticity of supply, E_s	unit elasticity
coefficient of elasticity	

SOLVED EXAMPLE PROBLEMS

Let's reuse a demand example from the previous chapter.

Remember the regional market for housing. Demand for single detached homes depends on the price of the house, P_H, consumer income, N, and the price of a related good, townhouses, P_T. The demand equation is:

$$Q_d = 0.2N + 0.05P_T - 0.01P_H.$$

Initially, average consumer income is N = $50 000 and the average price of townhouses is $285 000. Making these substitutions we get:

$Q_d = 0.2N + 0.05P_T - 0.01P_H$

$Q_d = 0.2(50\ 000) + 0.05(285\ 000) - 0.01P_H$

$Q_d = 10\ 000 + 14\ 250 - 0.01P_H$

$Q_d = 24\ 250 - 0.01P_H$ This is our current demand equation.

1. What is the price elasticity of demand when the price of housing changes from $250 000 to $300 000?

   We need to find the corresponding values of Q_d.

   When P = 250 000, Q_d = 21 750

   When P = 300 000, Q_d = 21 250

   $E_p = (\Delta Q/Q)/(\Delta P/P)$

   $= \{(300\ 000 - 250\ 000)/250\ 000\}/\{(21\ 250 - 21\ 750)/21\ 750\}$

   $= 0.20/-0.023$

   $= -8.7$ We take the absolute value, so E_p = 8.7, elastic.

2. What is the point elasticity of demand when the price of housing is $250 000?

   From the previous question, when P = 250 000, Q_d = 21 750

   The |slope| of the demand curve is 0.01. This is dQ/dP.

   $E_p = dQ/dP \star P/Q$

   $= 0.01 \star (250\ 000/21\ 750)$

   $= 0.11$

3. Why is there such a big difference in the value of the coefficient E_p from question 1 to question 2?

   In question 1, the price changes used for the calculations covered a big range, $50 000 to be exact. When we calculate point elasticity, we use a marginal change in price. If we used the percentage change formula with a $1 change in price:

   When P = 250 001, Q_d = 21 749.99

   $E_p = (\Delta Q/Q)/(\Delta P/P)$

   $= \{(0.01)/21\ 750\}/\{1/250\ 000\}$

   $= 0.11$ The same as our point elasticity coefficient value. Not a coincidence.

4. Suppose income changes from $50 000 to $60 000. What is the income elasticity of demand for housing when price is $250 000?

   When N = 50 000 and P_H = 250 000, Q_d is 21 750 (what we calculated above)

   When N = 60 000 and P_H = 250 000, holding P_T constant at $285 000, Q_d is

   $Q_d = 0.2N + 0.05P_T - 0.01P_H$

   $Q_d = 0.2(60\ 000) + 0.05(285\ 000) - 0.01(250\ 000)$

   $= 23\ 750$

   $E_N = (\Delta Q/Q)/(\Delta N/N)$

   $= \{(23\ 750 - 21\ 750)/21\ 750\}/\{(60\ 000 - 50\ 000)/50\ 000\}$

   $= 0.092/0.20$

   $= 0.46$ A normal good since $E_N > 0$ but income inelastic since $E_N < 1$.

5. Suppose $N = 50\ 000$ and $P_H = 250\ 000$. If the price of townhouses decreases from $285 000 to $260 000, what is the cross price elasticity of the demand for housing?

When $N = 50\ 000$, $P_H = 250\ 000$ and $P_T = 285\ 000$, $Q_d = 21\ 750$ (our original calculation)

When $P_T = 260\ 000$, $Q_d = 0.2N + 0.05P_T - 0.01P_H$

$$Q_d = 0.2(50\ 000) + 0.05(260\ 000) - 0.01(250\ 000)$$

$$= 20\ 500$$

$E_{a,b} = (\Delta Q \text{ of housing}/Q \text{ of housing})/(\Delta P \text{ of townhomes}/P \text{ of townhomes})$

$= \{(20\ 500 - 21\ 750)/21\ 750\}/\{(260\ 000 - 285\ 000)/285\ 000\}$

$= -0.057/-0.088$

$= 0.65\ E_{a,b} > 0$ so the goods are substitutes.

6. Market supply is $Q_s = 6P + 100$

a) What is the elasticity of demand when price changes from $10 to $20?

When $P = 10$, $Q_s = 160$

When $P = 20$, $Q_s = 220$

$Es = (\Delta Q/Q)/(\Delta P/P)$

$= \{(220 - 160)/160\}/\{(20 - 10)/10\}$

$= 0.375 / 1$

$= 0.375\ E_s < 1$ so supply is price inelastic.

b) What is the point elasticity of supply when $P = \$10$?

When $P = 10$, $Q_s = 160$. The slope of supply is $dQ/dP = 6$.

$E_s = dQ/dP \star P/Q = 6\star(10/160) = 0.375$

PROBLEMS

You may have noticed by now that elasticity calculations are fairly mechanical and therefore tedious. Here are a few practice questions anyway.

The following table shows values for Q_d of Good X at various prices, incomes and prices of a related Good Y. The equation of the demand curve is $Q_d = 100 - 2P$.

Q_d	P_x	N	P_y
80	10	10	5
60	20	5	10

1. Using the percentage change relationship, what is the price elasticity of demand for Good X when price changes from $10 to $20?

2. What is the point elasticity of demand for Good X when price is $10?

3. What is the income elasticity of demand for Good X over the range presented above?

4. What is the cross-price elasticity of demand for Good X? Is Good Y a substitute or a complement for Good X?

   The equation for the supply of Good X is given by $Q_s = 3P$.

5. What is the elasticity of supply over the range of prices going from \$10 to \$20? Use the percentage change formula.

6. What is the point elasticity of supply when price equals \$10?

7. What is the point elasticity of supply when price equals \$20?

8. If $Q_d = 100 - 2P$ and $Q_s = 3P$, which curve is relatively more elastic?

SOLUTIONS

The following table shows values for Q_d of Good X at various prices, incomes and prices of a related Good Y. The equation of the demand curve is $Q_d = 100 - 2P$.

Q_d	P_x	N	P_y
80	10	10	5
60	20	5	10

1. Using the percentage change relationship, what is the price elasticity of demand for Good X when price changes from $10 to $20?

   $E_p = | (\Delta Q/Q)/(\Delta P/P) |$

   $= | \{(60 - 80)/80\}/\{(20 - 10)/10\} |$

   $= 0.25/1$

   $= 0.25$ $E_p < 1$ so demand is inelastic

2. What is the point elasticity of demand for Good X when price is $10?

   |Slope| is 2. When P = 10, $Q_d = 80$

   $E_p = 2 * 10/80$

   $= 0.25$

3. What is the income elasticity of demand for Good X over the range presented above?

   $E_N = (\Delta Q/Q)/(\Delta N/N)$

   $= \{(60 - 80)/80\}/\{(5 - 10)/10\}$

   $= -0.25/-0.5$

   $= 0.5$ $0 < E_N < 1$ so demand is income inelastic and Good X is a normal good.

4. What is the cross-price elasticity of demand for Good X? Is Good Y a substitute or a complement for Good X?

   $E_{x,y} = (\Delta Qx/Qx)/(\Delta Py/Py)$

   $= \{(60 - 80)/80\}/\{(10 - 5)/5\}$

   $= -0.25/1$

   $= -0.25 < E_{x,y} < 0$ so Good X and Good Y are complements (weak complements since the coefficient is only -0.25).

   The equation for the supply of Good X is given by $Q_s = 3P$.

5. What is the elasticity of supply over the range of prices going from $10 to $20? Use the percentage change formula.

   When P = 10, $Q_s = 30$. When P = 20, $Q_s = 60$.

   $E_s = (\Delta Q/Q)/(\Delta P/P)$

   $= \{(60 - 30)/30\}/\{(20 - 10)/10\}$

   $= 1 / 1$

   $= 1$ $E_s = 1$ so supply is unit inelastic.

6. What is the point elasticity of supply when price equals $10?

   Slope is 3. When P = 10, $Q_s = 30$

   $E_s = 3 * 10/30$

   $= 1$ $E_s = 1$ so supply is unit inelastic.

7. What is the point elasticity of supply when price equals $20?

Slope is 3. When P = 20, Q_s = 60

E_s = 3 * 20/60

= 1 E_s = 1 so supply is unit inelastic.

NOTICE: E_s = 1 at any point on this supply curve because it is a ray through the origin. It doesn't matter what the slope is.

8. If Q_d = 100 − 2P and Q_s = 3P, which curve is relatively more elastic?

Compare the slopes of the two curves. To do this, rewrite the equations in terms of P = f(Q) because those are the equations we actually graph. Whichever curve has the smaller (flatter) slope is the more elastic curve.

Demand: 2P = 100 − Q so P = 50 − 0.5Q |Slope| = 0.5

Supply: 3P = Q so P = Q/3 Slope = 0.33

The supply curve is flatter than the demand curve, so supply is more elastic.

CHAPTER 5
Welfare, Externalities & Public Goods

MAIN CONCEPTS AND DEFINITIONS

Economic Welfare: benefits consumers and firms receive by participating in the market (buying and selling).

Consumer Surplus: the benefit consumers receive when the price they pay for a good is less than the dollar amount value they place on the good.

Normally we read the demand curve as "here's the price—how much do consumers want to buy at that price?" But we can also read it in the other direction as "here's the available quantity—how much would consumers pay per good to buy that much?" In this sense, the demand curve depicts the **value** consumers place on a good; it shows the maximum amount they would pay to purchase a given quantity of the good.

Consumers have a **reservation price**—a willingness to buy—which is the *highest* price they are willing to pay for a good. This price indicates how much they *value* the good.

We know what that reservation price is when we look at the demand curve. The demand curve is our price curve; it tells us the highest price (and therefore the value) that consumers are willing to pay when different quantities of a good are available. Consumer surplus for the market is the area under the demand curve (value) above the price consumers pay (market price).

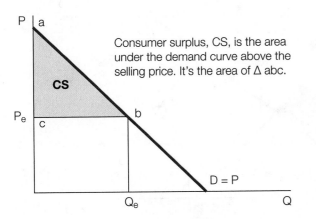

Consumer surplus, CS, is the area under the demand curve above the selling price. It's the area of Δ abc.

Producer Surplus: the benefit sellers receive when the price they receive is more than the bottom-dollar price they need to produce and offer their good for sale.

We usually read the supply curve as "here's the price—how much are firms willing and able to supply at that price?" How much depends on producers' costs. The supply curve tells us the lowest price producers will accept to supply a specified amount; this price has to cover the producers' costs to produce that quantity.

Producers have a reservation price—a willingness to sell—which is the *least* amount of money they are willing to take to sell a good. This price is a reflection of their costs of production (high-cost producers will need higher prices to sell their output without losing money).

We can see producers' reservation prices by looking at the supply curve. The supply curve reflects the firms' costs; it indicates what the price has to be in order for producers to supply the good. Producer surplus is the area under the price producers receive (market price) above the supply curve (producers' reservation prices).

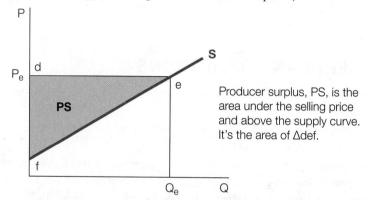

Producer surplus, PS, is the area under the selling price and above the supply curve. It's the area of △def.

Total Surplus = Consumer Surplus + Producer Surplus. It measures the total benefit enjoyed by consumers and producers in the market. Since it's everything under the demand curve and above the supply curve, you can think of total surplus as the value to consumers (demand) minus the cost to producers (supply).

Total surplus is maximized in a perfectly competitive equilibrium where the market is left to operate freely.

IMPORTANT: **You can only get surplus if you actually buy or sell a good.**

Total Surplus = CS + PS

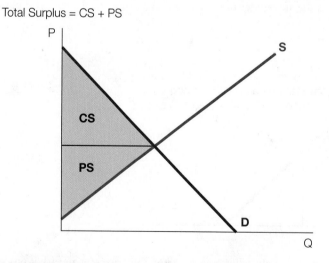

DEADWEIGHT LOSS IN TOTAL SURPLUS

Deadweight Loss, DWL: a loss in total surplus when the quantity traded is less than the competitive equilibrium quantity.

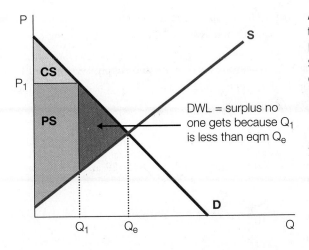

At $Q_1 < Q_e$, price is P_1. CS is the area of the small triangle (below D and above P_1). PS is everything under P_1 and above the S curve, but only up to Q_1. The difference $Q_e - Q_1$ is not being produced, so no buyers can get surplus for those goods because they're not buying anything and no producers can get any surplus for those goods because they're not selling anything. The area of the brown triangle represents a deadweight loss in surplus: surplus no one gets anymore because fewer goods are produced and sold.

DWL = surplus no one gets because Q_1 is less than eqm Q_e

You may also incur a deadweight loss if there is overproduction in the market. We'll see an example in the next section.

EXAMPLE

As we have seen in this chapter, consumer surplus (CS) is the area under the demand curve above the price consumers actually pay for the good. Similarly, producer surplus (PS) is the area under the price they actually receive for the good above the supply curve. In a competitive market equilibrium, total surplus is maximized.

CS and PS are the areas of triangles when we are in a competitive equilibrium. If we have the equations for demand and supply, we can easily find the areas of these triangles by finding equilibrium price and quantity and the values of the P-intercepts for our demand and supply curves.

The area of a triangle is calculated as Area = 1/2 bh, where b is the length of the base of the triangle and h is the height of the triangle.

Consider the following diagram where we are in a competitive equilibrium:

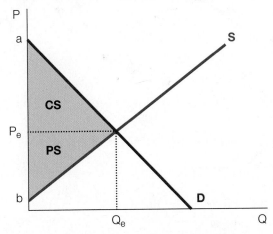

CS is the area under the demand curve above P_e. The base of this triangle is the length Q_e. The height of this triangle is $a - P_e$. The area of this triangle is $1/2 \star Qe \star (a - P_e)$, and that is the dollar value of CS.

PS is the area under P_e above the supply curve. The base of this triangle is the length Q_e. The height of this triangle is $P_e - b$. The area of this triangle is $1/2 \star Qe \star (P_e - b)$ and that is the dollar value of PS.

If we have the equations for demand and supply, we can find P_e and Q_e and also find the values for the intercepts a and b. Then we can calculate a numerical value for CS and PS for our given market.

EXAMPLE

Market demand for stuff is given by $Q_d = 80 - 2P$ and market supply for stuff is given by $Q_s = P - 10$.

In equilibrium $Q_d = Q_s$:

$80 - 2P = P - 10$

$90 = 3P$

$P_e = 30$ and $Q_e = 20$

Now we need the price intercepts for our demand and supply curves. To find these values, set $Q = 0$ in each equation.

For our demand curve, $0 = 80 - 2P$ so the P-intercept is 40 (that would be a in our diagram).

For our supply curve, $0 = P - 10$ so the P-intercept is 10 (that would be b in our diagram).

For consumer surplus: the base of the triangle is 20 and the height is $40 - 30 = 10$.
$CS = \frac{1}{2} \star 20 \star 10 = \$100$.

For producer surplus: the base of the triangle is 20 and the height is $30 - 10 = 20$.
$PS = \frac{1}{2} \star 20 \star 20 = \$200$.

Total surplus (TS) is $\$100 + \$200 = \$300$.

Here's what we did:

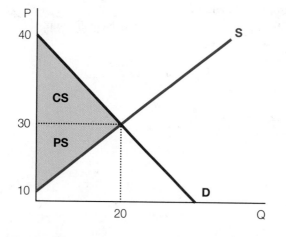

EXTERNALITIES

We just saw how buyers and sellers can enjoy benefits when they participate in market transactions. Sometimes these benefits—and sometimes costs—accrue to individuals who have nothing to do with an actual market transaction.

Positive Externality: a benefit enjoyed by individuals even though they did not pay to receive it. Example: Your neighbour goes to a garden centre, <u>buys</u> a big tree and <u>you</u> enjoy the shade the tree casts in your yard every afternoon. This is a **positive externality in consumption**. Example: A beekeeper farms bees to <u>produce</u> honey, but the bees also pollinate the beautiful flowers that <u>you</u> enjoy in the park next door. This is a **positive externality in production**.

Negative Externality: a cost suffered by individuals for which they are not compensated. Example: Your neighbour <u>buys</u> a dog from a breeder and its barking keeps <u>you</u> awake all night. This is a **negative externality in consumption**. Example: A local factory emits nasty chemicals into the lake during the <u>production</u> of steel and pollutes the water so <u>you</u> can't swim anymore. This is a **negative externality in production**.

Marginal Private Benefit, MPB: We saw earlier in this chapter that consumers have a reservation price, the maximum amount they would pay to purchase a given quantity of the good. What quantity? Marginal private benefit is the maximum price someone would pay to consume *one more unit of the good*. Generally, MPB decreases as more of the good is consumed (the Law of Demand and hence the downward sloping demand curve). So, the demand curve is also the marginal private benefit curve.

Marginal Private Cost, MPC: We also saw earlier in this chapter that producers have a reservation price, the lowest price they will take to produce a certain quantity of a good. To produce more costs producers more; the supply curve gives the added cost to producers of producing an additional good. So, the supply curve is the marginal private cost curve or marginal cost, MC, for short. It's the addition to the firm's *total* cost from producing *one more good*.

When there are no externalities, in the competitive equilibrium MPB = MPC and the market outcome is efficient. When there are externalities that are unaccounted for, the market outcome is not efficient. Negative externalities result in too much output and positive externalities result in too little output produced.

EXAMPLE: MARKET FOR STEEL

The production of steel also leads to air and water pollution. The cost of steel to society, **marginal *social* cost, MSC**, is greater than just the private cost borne by producers of steel because we add in the cost of the accompanying pollution.

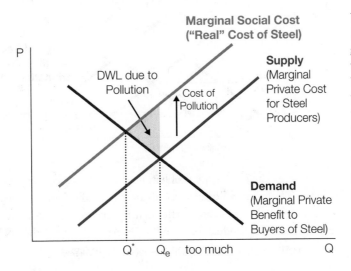

There's a DWL because MSC—the "real" cost—is greater than the MPB – the value to the buyers of steel. Whenever costs > value, that's negative surplus. It would be subtracted from total surplus, making TS less than what it would be at the "correct" Q* equilibrium—a DWL in surplus.

EXAMPLE: MARKET FOR EDUCATION

Education benefits not only those who go to school; all of society benefits by having an educated, more productive population. The value of education to everyone, **marginal** *social* **benefit, MSB**, is greater than just the private benefit to those who receive the education.

There's a DWL because the quantity produced is less than what it should be at the "correct" Q* equilibrium, making TS less than what it should be—a DWL in surplus.

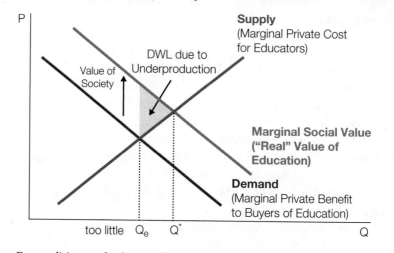

Externalities can be **internalized**: The market participants who caused the externality can be made to include the costs or benefits of their actions and adjust their decisions accordingly. For instance, the government could tax steel producers an amount that covers the cost of the pollution and shifts the supply curve back so that the optimal outcome results. Once the tax is levied, the MSC and the MPC curves are now the same curve.

Another instance is that the government can subsidize schools and increase the supply of education so that the optimal number of educated persons results:

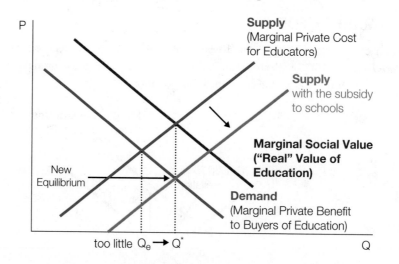

Solving the externality problem may not always require government intervention. The **Coase Theorem** postulates that if the bargaining costs are small and property rights are well-defined, the individual parties may be able to come to a solution themselves. **Property rights** give an individual (or even the government) the authority to own and use a resource any way they choose (providing the actions are legal). If you want recompense for putting up with a noisy dog, you have to know who is the legal owner of the dog so you can go after the person responsible for the externality.

PUBLIC GOODS

Sometimes the presence of externalities can deter a private producer from supplying a good. There could be the problem of a **free rider**: someone who enjoys the benefit of a good but avoids paying for it.

For example, the city puts on a fireworks show for Canada Day. Instead of buying a ticket to enter the park, you stand outside the fence, look up, and enjoy the show without paying. A private firm would realize that ticket sales would be minimal and not put on the show because it probably wouldn't be profitable. But residents enjoy the fireworks show, and it will be provided as a public good.

A **public good** is a good or service provided by the government for society to consume free of charge. Since there are no prices, there is no price mechanism to ensure that resources are efficiently allocated.

We can classify goods by the presence or absence of 2 characteristics:

Excludability: someone can be prevented from using the good.

Rivalry: if someone is using a good, others' ability to use that same good diminishes.
There are 4 kinds of goods based on the above criteria.

- **Public Goods**: non-excludable, non-rival. Example: a lighthouse. Non-excludable because you can't keep ships from using it; non-rival because the use of the light by one ship does not detract from the ability of another ship to benefit from the light.

- **Private Goods**: excludable and rival. Example: your house. Excludable because if you don't have the money or can't get a mortgage, you can't buy the house; rival in that your ownership means that someone else can't own that same house at the same time.

- **Common Goods**: non-excludable and rival. Example: non-toll highways. Non-excludable because you can't keep traffic off the roads; rival in that the more cars on the road, the greater the congestion due to traffic volume and the more unpleasant the drive.

- **Club Goods**: excludable and non-rival. Example: satellite television. Excludable because if you don't subscribe and pay your bill, you can't get satellite TV; non-rival in that you watching your favourite show doesn't impede other subscribers from watching and enjoying their shows.

How does the government decide if and what goods to publicly provide? Normally, if the benefits outweigh the costs, a good should be provided. Costs can be straightforward to calculate, but in the absence of prices, it may be impossible to value the benefits. Consider national defence, police and fire services, and parklands. These publicly provided goods and services have great value to the citizens who benefit from them. It may be difficult, if not impossible, to assign a precise dollar *value* but the *costs* are calculable (and made public in the providing government's annual budgets).

TRAGEDY OF THE COMMONS

Tragedy of the commons refers to the misuse or overuse of common (public) property by individuals acting in their own best interest while ignoring the interests of the collective. Back in medieval times, locals would bring their cows to a common pasture to graze.

As the number of cows brought to graze increased, the grass would be eaten up, leaving less grass for other cows. Locals acting in their best interest (making sure their cows were fed) overused the commons and eventually the pasture disappeared, hurting everyone. The governing locals could have limited the number of cows allowed to graze or, even better, sectioned off the pasture for each farmer, creating private property.

Today, governments try to avoid the tragedy of the commons by regulating the use of common resources. Wildlife is protected, hunters require licences and can only hunt at specified times, toll roads eliminate free riders and reduce traffic congestion and polluters are taxed, to name a few remedies.

KEY TERMS

economic welfare	marginal private cost, MPC
consumer surplus	marginal *social* cost, MSC
value	marginal *social* benefit, MSB
reservation price	internalized
producer surplus	Coase Theorem
total surplus	property rights
deadweight loss, DWL	free rider
positive externality	public good
positive externality in consumption	excludability
positive externality in production	rivalry
negative externality	private goods
negative externality in consumption	common goods
negative externality in production	club goods
marginal private benefit, MPB	tragedy of the commons

SOLVED EXAMPLE PROBLEMS

The diagram below illustrates the market for outdoor concert tickets in a park in the middle of a residential area in Lewiston. Ticket prices are measured in dollars (the grid is drawn for $2.50 increments) and ticket quantities are measured in *thousands*. The locals are not happy about the increased traffic congestion and noise that accompany each concert.

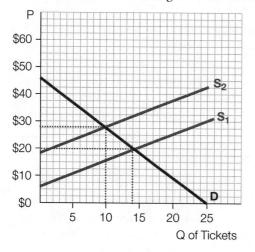

1. Which supply curve represents the marginal private cost of the concerts? What is the market equilibrium?

   Marginal private costs, because they do not reflect the costs of the negative externality, are lower than the marginal social costs. S_1 is the MPC curve.

   Equilibrium (Q, P) is (14 000, $20).

2. What is the value of consumer surplus at market equilibrium?

   Consumer surplus, CS, is the area under the demand curve above the market equilibrium price. $CS = 0.5(45 - 20)(14\,000) = \$175\,000$

3. What is the value of producer surplus at market equilibrium?

   Producer surplus, PS, is the area under the market equilibrium price above the supply curve. $PS = 0.5(20 - 5)(14\,000) = \$105\,000$

4. What is the cost of the externality per concert ticket?

   The cost per concert ticket is the vertical distance between the MPC curve and S_2 (which must be the MSC curve because it's higher and reflects higher costs that include the costs of the traffic and noise): $12.50 per concert ticket sold.

5. What is the socially optimal number and price of concert tickets?

   The socially optimal equilibrium occurs at (Q, P) = (10 000, $27.50).

6. What is the deadweight loss due to the externality?

   $DWL = 0.5(12.50)(4000) = \$25\,000.$

The following diagram depicts the market for cough medicine in a small town. The quantity of cough medicine is measured in bottles sold per week; price is measured in dollars. The townspeople are happier and healthier because people who have colds and flus buy and take the medicine and reduce the spread of infection.

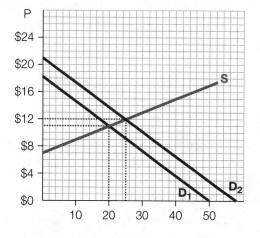

1. Which supply curve represents the marginal private benefit of cough medicine? What is the market equilibrium?

2. What is the value of consumer surplus at market equilibrium?

3. What is the value of producer surplus at market equilibrium?

4. What is the cost of the externality per bottle of cough medicine?

5. What is the socially optimal number and price of cough medicine?

6. What is the deadweight loss due to the externality?

SOLUTIONS

1. Which supply curve represents the marginal private benefit of cough medicine? What is the market equilibrium?

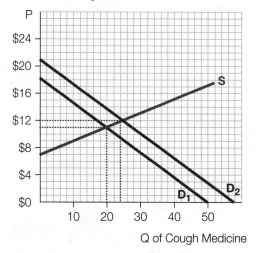

   Marginal private benefits, because they do not reflect the benefits of the positive externality, are lower than the marginal social benefits. D_1 is the MPB curve.

   Equilibrium (Q, P) is (20, $11).

2. What is the value of consumer surplus at market equilibrium?

   Consumer surplus, CS, is the area under the demand curve above the market equilibrium price. CS = 0.5(18 − 11)(20) = $70.

3. What is the value of producer surplus at market equilibrium?

   Producer surplus, PS, is the area under the market equilibrium price above the supply curve. PS = 0.5(11 − 7)(20) = $40.

4. What is the cost of the externality per bottle of cough medicine?

   The cost per bottle of cough medicine is the vertical distance between the MPB curve and D_2 (which must be the MSB curve because it's higher and reflects higher value that includes the benefits of lower risk of catching something): $3.00 per bottle sold.

5. What is the socially optimal number and price of cough medicine?

   The socially optimal equilibrium occurs at (Q, P) = (24, $12.00).

6. What is the deadweight loss due to the externality?

   DWL = 0.5(3)(4) = $6.

CHAPTER 6
Government Policies

PRICE CONTROLS

When the government doesn't like the market equilibrium price, it can freeze the price level at an artificial amount that it thinks will result in a more equitable outcome for target members of the market.

If the government thinks a market equilibrium price is too high, it can impose a **price ceiling**: a legal maximum on the price that can be charged for the good. The price has to be lower than equilibrium price in order to be binding (effective). An example is a rent freeze where governments limit what landlords can charge as rent in order to make housing more affordable.

If the government thinks a market equilibrium price is too low, it can impose a **price floor**: a legal minimum on the price that can be charged for the good. The price has to be higher than equilibrium price in order to be binding (effective). An example is a floor price on wheat where governments increase what farmers receive for wheat in order to ensure farmers make at least a certain amount of money.

Price freezes lead to inefficiency in the market. Price ceilings lead to shortages, wasted resources, black markets, low-quality goods, and inefficient allocations to buyers. Price floors lead to excess supply, waste, unnecessarily high-quality goods, and inefficient allocations to producers. Both lead to deadweight losses in total surplus.

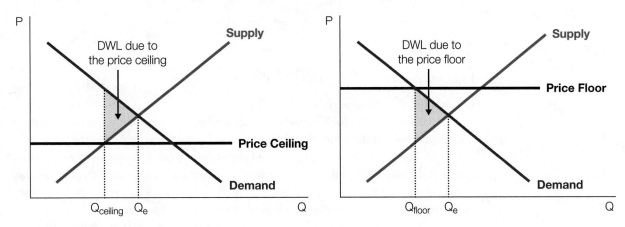

SALES TAXES

The government collects sales taxes as revenue toward the funding of public goods and projects. It can tax firms or consumers; it doesn't care who it taxes because the end result will be the same either way.

A tax on producers

Suppose we have current demand and supply equations and are told the government plans to levy (place) a per unit sales tax on firms.

Let t = the amount of the per unit tax.

The government doesn't care about the equilibrium price level. It wants to receive the amount t on every unit sold regardless of the good's current selling price. In effect, this raises the cost of production for the firm at every price level. The supply curve shifts up (supply decreases) by the amount of the tax. There will be a new intersection of the after-tax supply curve and the unchanged demand curve leading to a new equilibrium. The new equilibrium price is higher and the equilibrium quantity traded is lower than before the tax.

The consumer pays the new equilibrium price, P_c. The firm collects P_c from the buyer and takes out the amount of the tax, t, to set aside and remit to the government. The firm is left with a price $P_f = P_c - t$. The government's tax revenue is $t*Q_{tax}$.

Because the after-tax quantity traded is less than the previous competitive equilibrium, there is a deadweight loss due to the tax.

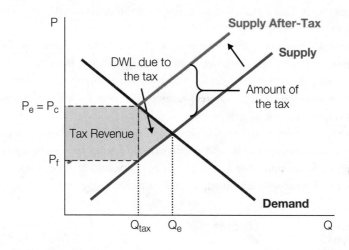

A tax on consumers

Now suppose that the government decides to levy the same tax, t, on consumers. Once again the government doesn't care about the equilibrium price level; it wants the amount t for every unit sold of the good. From the consumers' perspective, this raises the price they have to pay at every price level; the demand curve shifts down (demand decreases) by the amount of the tax. There will be a new intersection of the after-tax demand curve and the unchanged supply curve leading to a new equilibrium. The new equilibrium price is lower and the equilibrium quantity traded is lower than before the tax.

The consumer pays the firm $P_c = P_f + t$ (they pay the equilibrium price and add in the amount of the tax, t, that they have to pay). The firm collects P_c from the buyer and takes out the amount of the tax, t, to set aside and remit to the government on behalf of the consumer. The firm is left with the equilibrium price $P_f = P_c - t$. The government's tax revenue is $t*Q_{tax}$.

Because the after-tax quantity traded is less than the previous competitive equilibrium, again there is a deadweight loss due to the tax.

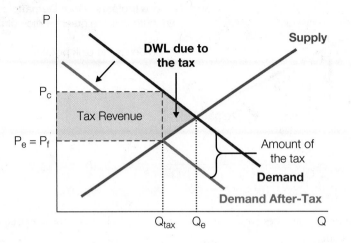

The government collects the same tax revenue, $t \star Q_{tax}$, regardless of who pays the tax, consumers or firms.

Notice that in either scenario, consumers pay a higher price and firms receive (end up with) a lower price than the pre-tax equilibrium price. Consumers and producers share the **burden** of the tax; how the burden is shared is what we call **tax incidence**.

ELASTICITY AND TAX INCIDENCE

Whichever side of the market is more inelastic (has the steeper curve) bears the larger burden of a tax.

The burden is the difference between the pre-tax equilibrium price and the higher, after-tax price paid by the consumer and lower, after-tax price received by the firm (producer).

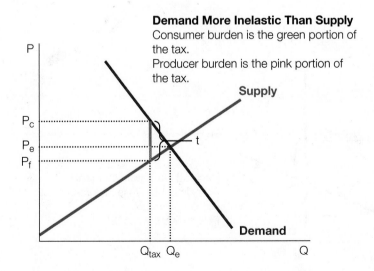

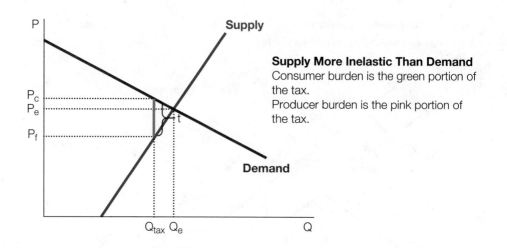

Supply More Inelastic Than Demand
Consumer burden is the green portion of the tax.
Producer burden is the pink portion of the tax.

There are also the extreme cases to consider. What if demand or supply is perfectly elastic or perfectly inelastic?

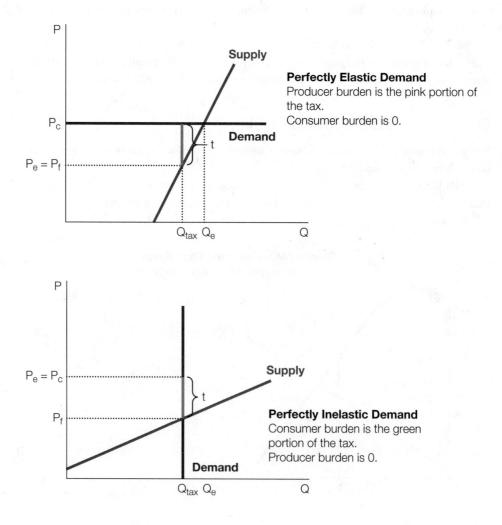

Perfectly Elastic Demand
Producer burden is the pink portion of the tax.
Consumer burden is 0.

Perfectly Inelastic Demand
Consumer burden is the green portion of the tax.
Producer burden is 0.

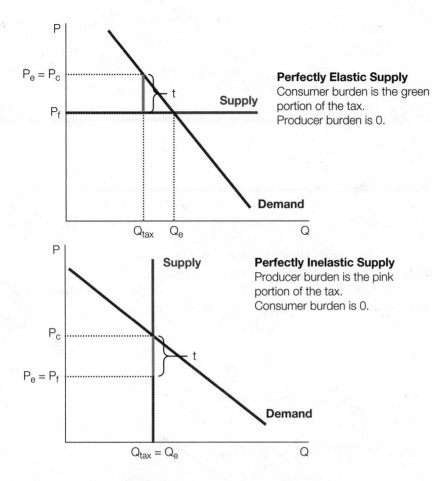

Perfectly Elastic Supply
Consumer burden is the green portion of the tax.
Producer burden is 0.

Perfectly Inelastic Supply
Producer burden is the pink portion of the tax.
Consumer burden is 0.

Total surplus with a sales tax

The tax reduces both consumer surplus and producer surplus. The tax revenue (made up of former consumer and producer surplus) will indirectly come back to market participants when the government spends it on public services. That's why the deadweight loss is only the area of the yellow triangle:

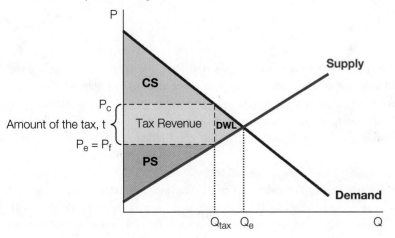

Elasticity and deadweight loss

The greater the elasticity of either or both demand and supply, the larger the deadweight loss. Why? Because elastic means Q_d and Q_s are more responsive to a change in price; when the tax changes the price, there will be greater decreases in the quantity traded and therefore greater deadweight losses.

SUBSIDIES

A **subsidy** is a government payment to firms in order to increase market output and/ or reduce prices paid by consumers. Think of subsidies as the opposite of taxes levied on producers. Subsidies shift the supply curve down (increase supply) by the amount of the per unit subsidy, resulting in a new equilibrium with more output and a lower equilibrium price. Consumers win by paying a lower price and having more output available and firms win by receiving the price consumers pay plus the per unit subsidy.

There is a deadweight loss due to the subsidy. The government has to spend money on the subsidy which comes out of what it would spend on social programs.

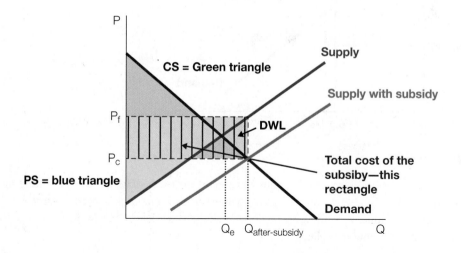

QUOTAS

A **quota** is a control on quantity. Governments will limit the legal amount of a good that can be sold because it wants to increase the price that sellers receive. Firms are issued quota licences that give them the legal right to produce a set maximum amount. Some examples of quotas are the number of taxis and limousines in a city, the limit on oil production set by OPEC, and the quota on Alaskan crab meant to curtail overfishing.

Limiting the quantity that can be produced and sold increases the price consumers pay for the now more scarce good. The quota is like a price floor with one important difference: By limiting the quantity that can be produced, there is no surplus production with a quota system. There is still a deadweight loss because the quota quantity is less than the competitive equilibrium outcome.

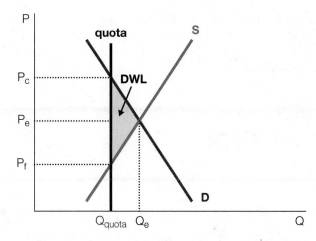

Consumers pay and firms receive price P_c. At the quota quantity, firms would have been happy to receive P_f. The difference between the two, $P_c - P_f$, is the value of the quota, called **quota rent**. It's the price someone would charge to sell their quota. The quota buyer would be able to produce and sell at P_c, pay the quota seller $P_c - P_f$ and happily end up with P_f.

THE ALGEBRA OF TAXATION

We have seen that whenever a unit sales tax is levied, regardless of whether it is levied on the consumer or on the producer, the consumer will pay a higher price and the firm will end up receiving a lower price than the equilibrium outcome (as long as both curves have elasticity greater than 0 and less than infinity). Now we can use algebra for our analysis.

First suppose that we are only told a tax has been levied and all we are given are the original demand and supply equations and a new after-tax equation (for either demand or supply, depending on whom the tax was levied). We solve for the new, after-tax equilibrium. Let's do an example:

The market for pizzas is represented by the following equations for demand and supply:

$$Q_d = 20 - 2P$$
$$Q_s = P - 1$$

In equilibrium,

$$Q_d = Q_s$$
$$20 - 2P = P - 1$$
$$P = \$7$$
$$Q = 6$$

Now suppose a tax on trans fats results in a $3 tax per pizza for pizza firms. The new supply curve is

$$Q_s = P - 4$$

For consumers, P_c is determined where the new $Q_s = Q_d$:

$$P - 4 = 20 - 2P$$
$$P = \$8$$

Since the firm has to pay the tax, it will end up with $5 for each pizza sold (the consumer pays them $8 and the firm has to send $3 of that to the government for the tax).

To find Q, substitute P = 8 into either the new Q_s or Q_d: (I'll use the new Q_s.)

$$Q_s = P - 4$$

$$Q_s = 4$$

So, with the tax, only 4 pizzas are traded in the market.

The government's tax revenue is $3 ⋆ 4 = $12.

Here's what it looks like:

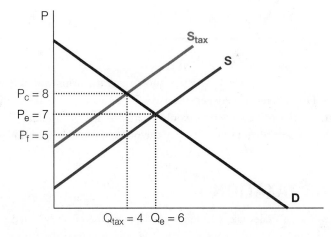

Now consider that we have current demand and supply equations and are told the amount of the unit tax. As we did before, let t = the amount of the per unit tax.

If the tax is placed on the consumer, the price the consumer will pay will be $P_c = P_f$ + t (the price the firm receives plus the tax). We substitute this into the demand curve. The firm will receive P_f. We use P_f in the supply curve. Now we solve for equilibrium Q and P_f. Just add the tax, t, to P_f and that is what the consumer pays. The government's tax revenue is t ⋆ Q.

If the tax is placed on the firm, the firm will end up with $P_f = P_c - t$ (the price the consumer pays minus the tax which it must remit to the government). We substitute this into the supply curve. The consumer will just pay P_c and we use this in the demand curve. Now we solve for equilibrium Q and P_c. Just subtract the tax, t, from P_c and that is what the firm ends up receiving.

EXAMPLE

In a competitive market, market supply for a good is Q = 3P and market demand is given as Q = 10 − 2P.

In equilibrium,   3P = 10 − 2P   so P = 2 and equilibrium quantity is Q = 6.

Now the government imposes a $0.50 per unit tax on consumers of the good.

The consumer pays $P_c = P_f + 0.50$ (the price the firm receives plus the tax).

The firm receives P_f.

The new equilibrium is $3P_f = 10 - 2 (P_f + 0.50)$

$$3P_f = 10 - 2P_f - 1$$

$$5P_f = 9$$

$$P_f = 1.80$$

So the firm receives $1.80 and the consumer pays $1.80 + the 0.50 tax = $2.30.

Now, let's reverse it and place the tax on firms.

The firm will end up with $P_f = P_c - 0.50$ (the price the consumer pays minus the tax which it must remit to the government).

The new equilibrium is $3(P_c - 0.50) = 10 - 2P_c$

$$3P_c - 1.50 = 10 - 2P_c$$

$$5P_c = 11.50$$

$$P_c = 2.30$$

So the consumer pays $2.30 and the firm remits the 0.50 tax to the government for a net take of $1.80, the same as before.

DEADWEIGHT LOSS

As we know, compared to the perfectly competitive outcome, whenever output is less than the competitive level of output, there will be a loss in total surplus. Since after-tax output is less than the competitive output, there will be a deadweight loss in surplus due to the tax.

Let's return to the first example, the pizza market. Here's what the deadweight loss looks like:

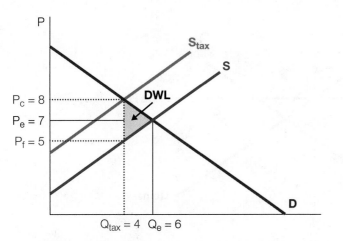

So all we need to find the area of the DWL triangle is the price consumers pay, price the firm receives, pre-tax equilibrium Q, and after-tax Q. Note that the base of the triangle, $P_c - P_f$, is just the amount of the tax, t.

DWL = 0.5(3)(2) = $3

HINT: Always draw the diagram so you know exactly what values you need to solve for DWL.

price ceiling
price floor
burden
tax incidence

subsidy
quota
quota rent

SOLVED EXAMPLE PROBLEMS

Market demand and supply for cases of beer are given by $Q_d = 960 - 4P$ and $Q_s = 20P$.

1. What is equilibrium (Q, P)?

   In equilibrium, $Q_d = Q_s$

   $$960 - 4P = 20P$$
   $$960 = 24P$$
   $$P = 40 \quad \text{and} \quad Q = 800$$

2. Suppose the government, concerned about excess consumption, decides to freeze the price of beer at $50 per case. What is the new quantity traded, and what is the dead-weight loss due to the price freeze?

   The price is frozen at a price above the market equilibrium, so it is a price floor. There will be excess supply at a price greater than equilibrium price; the short side of the market, Q_d, will dominate.

   At $P = 50$, $Q_d = 960 - 4(50) = 760$ cases.

   Let's draw it to see what deadweight loss will look like:

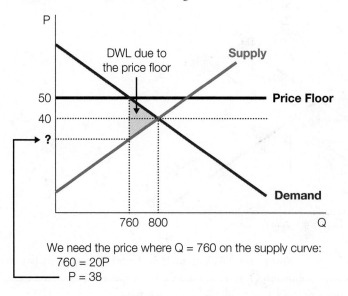

We need the price where $Q = 760$ on the supply curve:
$$760 = 20P$$
$$P = 38$$

We need the price where $Q = 760$ on the supply curve:

$$760 = 20P$$

$$P = 38$$

The DWL $= 0.5(50 - 38)(800 - 760) = \$240$

3. Instead of a price freeze, the government decides it wants to use the beer market to raise some tax revenue. It levies a tax of $10 per case on beer consumers.

    a) What is the equation of the demand curve with the tax included?

    Consumers will now pay $P_c = P_f + 10$. Producers will receive P_f.

    New demand is $Q_d = 960 - 4(P_f + 10)$
    $$Q_d = 960 - 4P_f - 40$$
    $$Q_d = 920 - 4P_f$$

    b) What is the new, after-tax equilibrium?

    Set the new demand equation equal to supply to get the new equilibrium price and quantity:

    $$920 - 4P_f = 20P_f$$
    $$920 = 24P_f$$
    $$P_f = 38.33$$
    $$Q_s = 20(38.33) = 766.60$$

    c) What price do consumers now pay?

    Consumers pay $P_c = P_f + 10 = 38.33 + 10 = \$48.33$

    d) Who has the larger burden of the tax?

    Consumers pay $8.33 ($48.33 − $40) more than before the tax.

    Firms receive $1.67 ($40 − $38.33) less than before.

    Consumers bear the larger burden.

    e) What is the deadweight loss due to the tax?

    Let's draw it first:

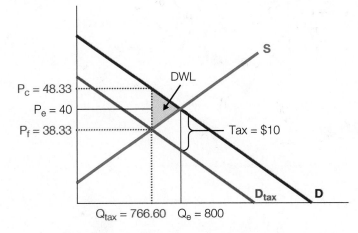

    $$DWL = 0.5(10)(800 - 766.60) = \$167.00$$

4. Suppose instead the government just decided to limit beer consumption and imposed a quota of 700 cases.

a) Draw the market with the quota and calculate the deadweight loss.

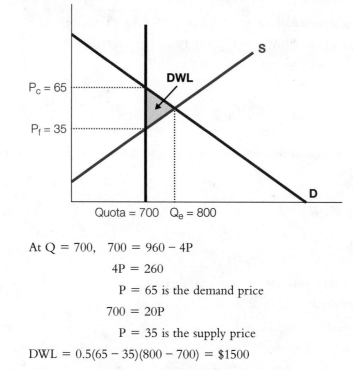

At Q = 700, 700 = 960 − 4P

$$4P = 260$$

P = 65 is the demand price

$$700 = 20P$$

P = 35 is the supply price

DWL = 0.5(65 − 35)(800 − 700) = $1500

b) If the government's only objective were to reduce the quantity sold, which policy would be better for the market: a price floor or a quota?

The price floor leads to surplus production and wasted resources. The quota, by limiting output, eliminates any surplus production and the waste associated with it. Either way there will be deadweight loss in surplus, but the quota is preferable.

In the market for nicotine gum to aid in the cessation of smoking, market demand and supply are given by $Q_d = 1200 - 200P$ and $Q_s = 100P$.

1. What is equilibrium price and quantity in the nicotine gum market?

2. The government sees the value of reducing the number of smokers and wants to subsidize nicotine gum producers so that they will make more gum available at a lower price to those trying to quit smoking. It offers a subsidy to producers of $2 per package of gum sold.

    a) Draw the market for the gum with the subsidy. What is the new equilibrium?
        HINT: A subsidy is like a negative tax.

    b) How much does the government spend on the subsidy?

c) What is the deadweight loss due to the subsidy?

3. Demand and supply in the market for bus fare in smaller city are given by $Q_d = 2400 - 500P$ and $Q_s = 300P$.

   a) What are equilibrium price and quantity?

   b) Suppose the local government feels that the fare is too high and decides to impose a price ceiling of $2.50 per bus trip. How many bus trips will be taken and what will be the deadweight loss in surplus due to the price ceiling? HINT: Draw it first.

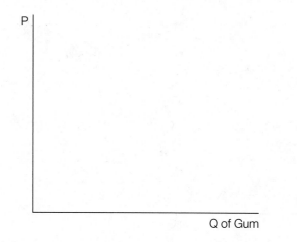

4. Demand and supply in the market for cases of soda pop is given by $Q_d = 288 - 10P$ and $Q_s = 2P$.

   a) What are equilibrium price and quantity?

b) Suppose the government is concerned about too much sugar in peoples' diets and decides to tax soda-pop sellers $3 per case. What is the equation of the new supply curve?

c) What is the new, after-tax equilibrium?

d) How much do consumers now pay and how much do sellers end up receiving?

e) What is the value of producer surplus both before and after the tax was levied? HINT: Draw it.

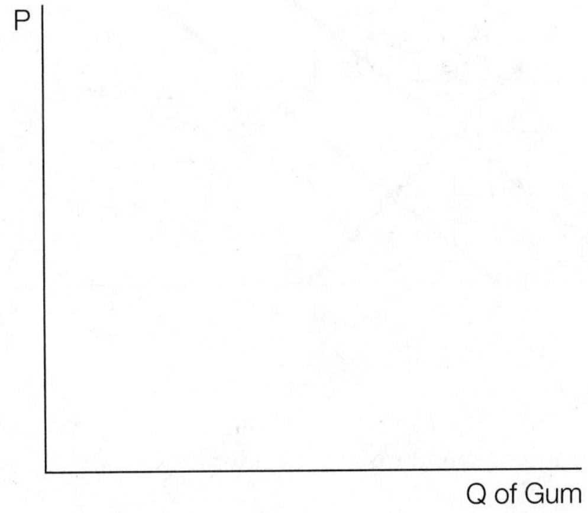

P

Q of Gum

f) What is the deadweight loss due to the tax? HINT: Draw it (you can use your diagram above).

SOLUTIONS

In the market for nicotine gum to aid in the cessation of smoking, market demand and supply are given by $Q_d = 1200 - 200P$ and $Q_s = 100P$.

1. What is equilibrium price and quantity in the nicotine gum market?

In equilibrium, $Q_d = Q_s$

$$1200 - 200P = 100P$$
$$1200 = 300P$$
$$P = 4 \quad \text{substitute into either } Q_d \text{ or } Q_s \text{ to get } Q$$
$$Q_s = 100(4) = 400 = Q_d = Q$$

2. The government sees the value of reducing the number of smokers and wants to subsidize nicotine gum producers so that they will make more gum available at a lower price to those trying to quit smoking. It offers a subsidy to producers of $2 per package of gum sold.

   a) Draw the market for the gum with the subsidy. What is the new equilibrium? HINT: A subsidy is like a negative tax.

Consumers pay P_c. Firms receive $P_f = P_c + 2$.
New supply curve equation:
$Q_s = 100(P_c + 2) = 100P_c + 200$
Set this equal to demand:
$1200 - 200P_c = 100P_c + 200$
$1000 = 300P_c$
$P_c = \$3.33$
$P_f = P_c + 2 = 3.33 + 2 = \$5.33$
To get the new quantity, substitute $P = \$3.33$ into either demand or the new supply curve:
$Q_s = 100(3.33) + 200 = 533 = Q_d$

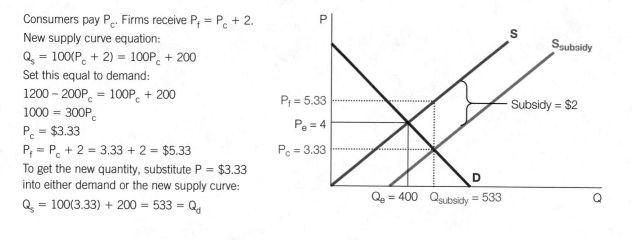

   b) How much does the government spend on the subsidy?
   $2 * 533 = \$1066$

   c) What is the deadweight loss due to the subsidy?
   DWL = 0.5(2)(133) = \$133

3. Demand and supply in the market for bus fare in a smaller city are given by $Q_d = 2400 - 500P$ and $Q_s = 300P$.

   a) What are equilibrium price and quantity?

In equilibrium, $Q_d = Q_s$

$$2400 - 500P = 300P$$
$$2400 = 800P$$
$$P = 3 \quad \text{substitute into either } Q_d \text{ or } Q_s \text{ to get } Q$$
$$Q_s = 300(3) = 900 = Q_d = Q$$

b) Suppose the local government feels that the fare is too high and decides to impose a price ceiling of $2.50 per bus trip. How many bus trips will be taken and what will be the deadweight loss in surplus due to the price ceiling? HINT: Draw it first.

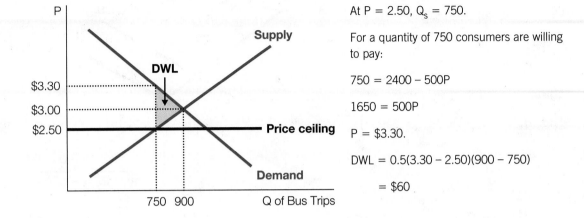

At P = 2.50, Q_s = 750.

For a quantity of 750 consumers are willing to pay:

$750 = 2400 - 500P$

$1650 = 500P$

P = $3.30.

DWL = 0.5(3.30 − 2.50)(900 − 750)

= $60

4. Demand and supply in the market for cases of soda pop is given by $Q_d = 288 - 10P$ and $Q_s = 2P$.

a) What are equilibrium price and quantity?

In equilibrium, $Q_d = Q_s$

$288 - 10P = 2P$

$288 = 12P$

$P = 24$ substitute into either Q_d or Q_s to get Q

$Q_s = 2(24) = 48 = Q_d = Q$

b) Suppose the government is concerned about too much sugar in peoples' diets and decides to tax soda pop sellers $3 per case. What is the equation of the new supply curve?

Firms will now receive $P_f = P_c - 3$. Consumers will pay P_c.

New supply is $Q_s = 2(P_c - 3)$

$Q_s = 2P_c - 6$

c) What is the new, after-tax equilibrium?

Set the new supply equation equal to demand to get the new equilibrium price and quantity:

$2P_c - 6 = 288 - 10P_c$

$294 = 12P_c$

$P_c = \$24.50$

$Q_s = 2(24.50) - 6 = 43$

d) How much do consumers now pay and how much do sellers end up receiving?

Consumers will pay $P_c = \$24.50$

Firms now receive $P_f = P_c - 3 = \$21.50$

e) What is the value of producer surplus both before and after the tax was levied? HINT: Draw it.

Before the tax:

PS = 0.5(24)(48) = $576.00

After the tax:

PS = 0.5(21.50)(43) = $462.25

*The diagram is not drawn to scale.

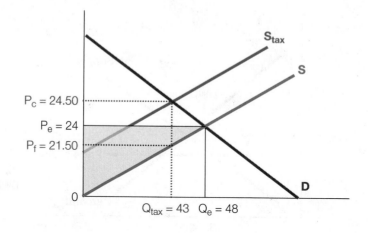

$P_c = 24.50$

$P_e = 24$

$P_f = 21.50$

0

$Q_{tax} = 43$ $Q_e = 48$

S_{tax}

S

D

f) What is the deadweight loss due to the tax? HINT: Draw it.

DWL = 0.5(3)(5) = $7.50

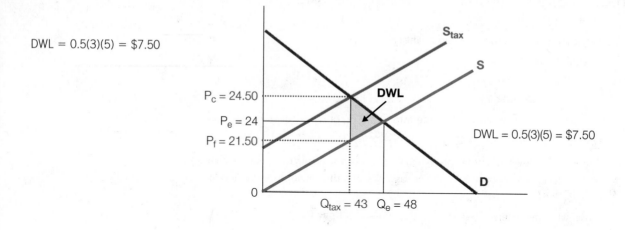

$P_c = 24.50$

$P_e = 24$

$P_f = 21.50$

0

$Q_{tax} = 43$ $Q_e = 48$

S_{tax}

DWL

S

DWL = 0.5(3)(5) = $7.50

D

CHAPTER 7
Production and Costs

MAIN CONCEPTS AND DEFINITIONS

The goal of virtually every firm is to maximize **profit**. Profit = total revenue − total costs. Using our abbreviations, Π = TR − TC. Maximizing profit means **minimizing costs**. Firms will try to produce the quantity of output that minimizes the cost of producing each good.

Total costs are calculated differently by an economist compared to an accountant. For an economist, total costs are total opportunity costs = explicit + implicit costs. We learned about opportunity costs in Chapter 1. Explicit costs are expenses for which you can get a receipt; these are the only ones that matter to an accountant. Implicit costs are for things you gave up (like a job working for someone else) but can't get a receipt for because you never really physically gave those things up. Because we include implicit costs, economic costs are bigger than accounting costs and therefore economic profits are smaller than accounting profits.

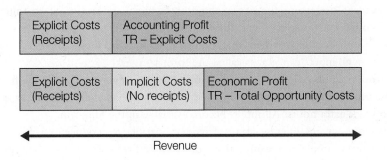

There are 3 categories of economic profit:

Positive economic profits are super high, unexpected profits for firms in that industry. These are the profits that attract entrepreneurs to the industry and induce new firms to enter the market.

Economic losses are negative profits. Firms that consistently earn losses will eventually leave the industry.

Normal economic profits are zero economic profits. These are the profits you'd expect for firms in that industry. These are nothing special, so no new firms will want to enter the market but no existing firms will be motivated to exit. Even though these are zero *economic* profits, the firm is still making an *accounting* profit. For example, you might be making $250 000 a year in accounting profit; if this is a decent return and typical for that industry, an economist will see that as zero economic profit.

Here's what zero economic profits look like:

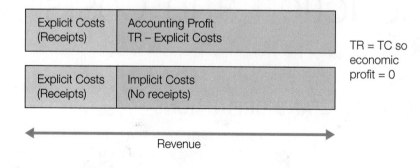

| Explicit Costs (Receipts) | Accounting Profit TR – Explicit Costs |
| Explicit Costs (Receipts) | Implicit Costs (No receipts) |

TR = TC so economic profit = 0

←————————— Revenue —————————→

PRODUCTION

Every firm has a **production function** which shows the relationship between the quantity of inputs used and the quantity of output they produce. We assume that firms have perfect information, know which technology is the best (most efficient) technology, and use that technology. The **technically efficient technology** produces the most output for any amount of inputs used.

We can characterize inputs as one of two types.

Fixed inputs: inputs that cannot vary in quantity for some period of time. Physical capital is a good example. Look around your classroom—it's a fixed input. There are only so many seats, so many projectors, the size of the room is fixed, and so on. These things can change given time, but at the moment, they're fixed.

The period of time in which at least one input is fixed is called the **short run**. The period of time when all inputs can vary is called the **long run**.

Variable inputs: inputs that can vary in quantity. Labour is a good example. If a firm wants to increase production, it can add a shift and hire new workers pretty quickly, or ask its employees to work extra hours. All inputs become variable in the long run.

Most goods require many different inputs, fixed and variable, to produce a final product. We'll keep it really simple and assume that our example firm uses only one variable input.

EXAMPLE: THE DONUT HUT

Tom is the manager of the Donut Hut. Everything Tom needs to sell snacks and beverages are provided daily by the franchise owner. It's not a huge space; there are 2 cash registers, 2 beverage stations, one big donut display, and one refrigerator, all fixed inputs that Tom doesn't have to worry about. Tom's only responsibility is to hire the labour needed to staff the store. So, the only input is labour, L, a variable input measured as the number of workers. Output, Q, is the number of customers served per hour. We often call output **total product, TP** (it's the same thing as Q).

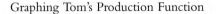

Graphing Tom's Production Function

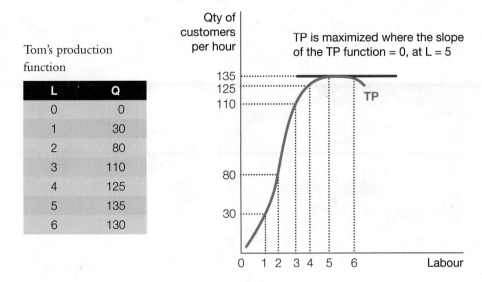

Tom's production function

L	Q
0	0
1	30
2	80
3	110
4	125
5	135
6	130

As the number of workers increases, the total number of customers served per hour increases. Every additional worker Tom hires adds to total output. But wait—each worker adds less to total output than the previous worker hired, and the sixth worker hired actually takes away from total output.

The change in total output as we change the number of variable inputs (in this example, only workers) is called **marginal product, MP**. Think of it as "If I add one more input, how much will my total output increase (or possibly decrease)?"

Marginal product is the rate of change in total output Q (or total product, TP) as the number of variable inputs changes. It is the slope of the total product function. The formula for marginal product is: $MP = \Delta Q / \Delta\#\text{of inputs}$.

Since Tom's only variable input is labour, the $MP_L = \Delta Q / \Delta L$.

Whenever we have fixed inputs, our variable inputs will have **diminishing marginal product**. This means that as we continue to add more of a variable input, the marginal product of each added input will be lower than the marginal product of the previous input added.

Imagine Tom's store. When he has one employee, she can serve 30 customers in an hour. If Tom adds another worker, that worker can serve customers, too, and help the first employee out. The second employee actually added 50 served customers to the total. If Tom adds a third employee, that employee adds 30 served customers to the total number served. It's a lower addition because there are only 2 cash registers; employee #3 helps out by making the coffee and packaging the donuts while the other two ring up the sales. If there were a third cash register, the third employee likely would have added more than 30 served customers to the total. A fourth employee can also help out by making beverages and keeping on top of other chores, but the store is not big and now employees start bumping into each other and spilling orders. The more employees Tom hires for the small store, the more congested it becomes and the workers really start tripping over each other. There may not be enough for everyone to do, so they're not adding to the total number of served customers. If Tom hired a sixth worker, there'd be so much congestion that everyone would be slowed down and the total number of customers served would actually decrease. All this explains why Tom's labour exhibits diminishing MP. We'll calculate it in the next table.

Tom may find it useful to think about the average product of his workers. **Average product, AP**, is the amount of <u>output per input</u>. **AP = Q/#of inputs**. For Tom, $AP_L = Q/L$.

Let's add MP and AP to our table:

L	Q	MP	AP
0	0		
1	30	30	30
2	80	50	40
3	110	30	36.7
4	125	15	31.3
5	135	10	27
6	130	−5	21.7

Notice that initially, both MP and AP rise but then start to fall (diminish).

When MP > AP, AP increases and when MP < AP, AP decreases. Think of what happens to your average grade when you add a grade that is higher or lower than your average grade. It's the same idea here.

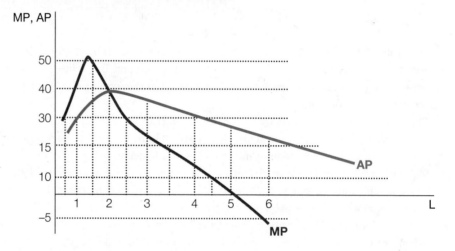

MP is a rate of change, so when we graph it, the values are plotted going from one quantity of labour to another. AP is just a number, so when we graph it the values are plotted at each corresponding quantity of labour.

When MP = AP, AP is at a maximum. Going from 5 to 6 workers, MP is negative. Tom would never hire labour where MP < 0. Notice that MP = 0 at L = 5. MP is the slope of total product; when MP = 0 the slope of the TP function is 0 and TP is at a maximum.

Usually we sketch nice, smooth curves like these:

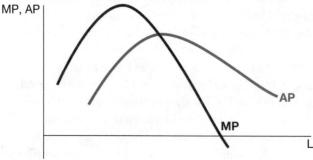

Maximum MP is the point of diminishing MP; maximum AP is the point of diminishing AP.

We can see that when MP > AP, AP increases and when MP < AP, AP decreases.

COSTS

SHORT-RUN COSTS

Total Fixed Costs, TFC: do <u>not</u> vary with the amount of output produced. Examples include loan payments, leases on equipment, mortgages, and salaried office staff. The bank doesn't care if you produce zero, 200, or 2000 goods per week; it wants your $10 000 loan payment on time regardless.

Average Fixed Costs, AFC: the fixed cost per unit of output. $AFC = TFC/Q$.

Total Variable Costs, TVC: <u>do</u> vary with the quantity of output produced. Examples include labour costs, raw material costs, shipping costs, and the like. If you want to increase your daily output, you'll need more raw materials and you'll need your workers to work more hours; your costs of variable inputs will increase as output increases.

Average Variable Costs, AVC: The variable cost per unit of output. $AVC = TVC/Q$.

Total Cost = Total Fixed Costs + Total Variable Costs or TC = TFC + TVC for short.

Average Total Cost, ATC: the total cost per unit of output. $ATC = TC/Q$.

Average Total Cost = AFC + AVC

Marginal Cost, MC: the addition to total cost from producing one more good. "If I produce one more good, by how much will my total cost of production increase (or possibly decrease)?" MC is the rate of change in TC when we increase output by one unit. It is the slope of the TC function. The formula for MC is $MC = \Delta TC/\Delta Q$.

Suppose Tom has fixed costs of $200 per hour. He pays each worker $11.00 per hour. The following table shows his total, average and marginal costs of production.

L	Q	MP	TFC	TVC	TC	MC	AFC	AVC	ATC
0	0		200	0	200				
1	30	30	200	11	211	0.37	6.67	0.37	7.04
2	80	50	200	22	222	0.22	2.50	0.28	2.78
3	110	30	200	33	233	0.37	1.82	0.30	2.12
4	125	15	200	44	244	0.73	1.60	0.35	1.95
5	135	10	200	55	255	1.1	1.48	0.41	1.89

When MP is at a maximum, MC is at a minimum, When MP diminishes, MC increases. This is not a coincidence. We can blame increasing MC on diminishing MP. Here's why:

Tom's first hire adds 30 served customers and costs Tom $11.00 per hour. Each of those first 30 customers cost Tom about $0.37 each in terms of his labour costs only. The second employee added 50 customers at her $11.00 per hour wage, costing Tom $0.22 each in labour costs of that employee. Worker #3 adds 30 served customers for a per customer cost of $0.37. Worker #4 adds 15 served customers, costing Tom $0.73 for each served customer at a wage of $11.00 for that worker. Tom pays each worker the same amount of money per hour; the more they produce, the lower the addition to total cost in terms of labour. The less they produce each hour, the more expensive each served customer becomes in terms of labour costs.

Notice that we have just seen that $MC_L = wage/MP_L$.

A typical firm's <u>total</u> cost curves look like these:

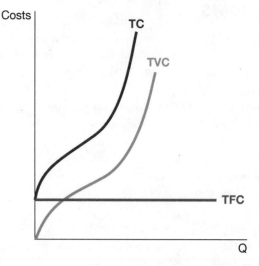

TFC are a horizontal line at the value of the fixed costs.

TVC begin to increase quickly as output increases.

TC is TVC moved up by the amount of TFC.

NOTE: The slope of TC = slope of TVC + slope of TFC. But the slope of TFC = 0, so the slope of TC = slope of TVC only. Since MC = slope of TC, MC = slope of TVC as well.

A typical firm's **short-run cost structure** (like Tom's) looks like this: (HINT: Know this well!)

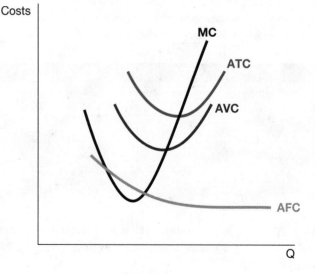

MC = ATC at minATC

MC = AVC at minAVC

When MC < AVC or ATC, AVC or ATC is falling.

When MC > AVC or ATC, AVC or ATC is rising.

AFC starts higher and decreases as Q rises.

ATC and AVC are u-shaped. AVC decreases when MP increases and rises when MP diminishes (as does MC). ATC is just AVC plus AFC, so ATC takes on the same u-shape.

LONG-RUN COSTS

In the long run (LR), firms can change anything and everything about how they produce their output. They can build any size factory, install as many or as few work stations as they like, paint the employee lounge any colour they want . . . everything is negotiable. In the LR, all inputs are variable. But know that once you build the factory, install the work stations, and paint the lounge walls olive green, you have just created some fixed inputs. That is, once you choose your ideal long run, you also choose its accompanying new short run (SR). So for every LR there's an associated SR with a set of SR cost curves.

Choosing a LR? A firm has an infinite number of choices it can make about production and capacity in the future. It has to determine the **scale** of its operations—how big does it want to be in the long run? The firm will plan where it wants to see itself down the road and make its decisions from there. Say a firm wants to remain folksy and family run; it will probably choose to produce a small but comfortable amount of output and therefore build a smaller, more manageable size plant. A firm on the verge of a technical breakthrough with plans to conquer the market will likely build a large capacity factory as its LR choice. Either firm, once it finalizes its LR production plan and builds the factory it needs, will incur a corresponding SR once the construction is done.

Consider a firm that is debating among 3 possible factory sizes—small, medium, and large—depending on how much it wants to produce in the LR. Of course, the firm wants to keep its costs minimized regardless of which size plant it chooses.

Let's graph the 3 SR ATC curves for each of the 3 LR factory sizes (we, and the firm, know what the SR cost curves look like for every factory size).

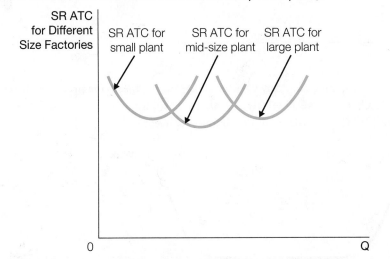

For whatever quantity of output it chooses to produce, the firm will use the factory size that produces it at least cost. If we only consider those parts of each SR ATC that minimize ATC for each factory size, we get a **long-run average cost curve, LRAC**, that looks like this:

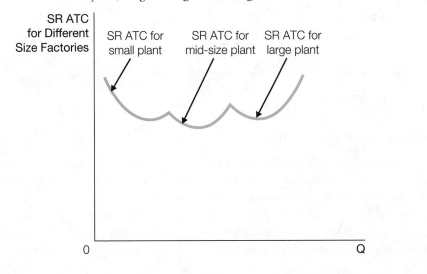

These are only 3 possible short runs. If we graphed an infinite number, the curve smoothens out and this is a firm's typical LRAC curve (in red):

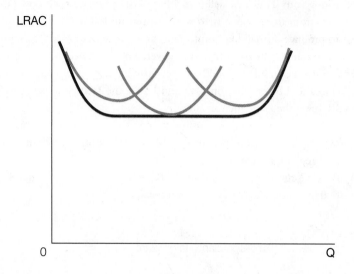

Check out the diagram below. Any Q between Q_1 and Q_2 means the firm is producing at minimum LRAC, so they are all **efficient scale** (size). Q_1 is the smallest amount needed to hit minimum LRAC—it is the point of minimum efficient scale.

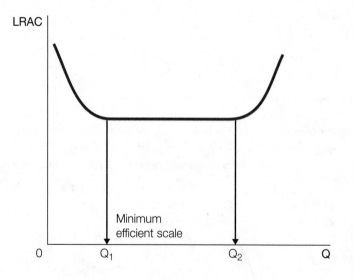

Scale economies in the long run

Depending on the firm's choice of output in the LR, increasing or decreasing that output level will have different impacts on LRAC based on where the firm is on the LRAC curve. We can separate the LRAC curve into 3 sections:

Increasing Returns to Scale, IRS: If you increase the quantity of output produced, LRAC falls (in our diagram, over the range from 0 to Q_1). Think of it as "If I double the amount of all my inputs, I'll get more than double the output." Two times the inputs

= 2 times TC. More than double the output means > 2 times Q. So the new LRAC = 2 * TC/more than 2Q = a LRAC *lower* than the original LRAC = LRAC falls. Firms would love to be in this position. You also may hear IRS referred to as economics of scale—same thing.

Decreasing Returns to Scale, DRS: If you increase the quantity of output produced, LRAC rises (in our diagram, for any output greater than Q_2). Think of it as "If I double the amount of all my inputs, I get less than double the output." Two times the inputs = 2 times TC. Less than double the output means < 2 times Q. So the new LRAC = 2 * TC/less than 2Q = a LRAC *higher* than the original LRAC = LRAC rises. Firms don't want to be in this position.

Constant Returns to Scale, CRS: There's no change in the quantity produced that will lead to any change in LRAC over a relevant range of output (in our diagram, from any amount greater than Q_1 to any amount lower than Q_2). Think of it as "If I double the amount of all my inputs, I get exactly double the output." Two times the inputs = 2 times TC. Double the output means 2 times Q. So the new LRAC = 2 * TC/2Q = TC/Q, a LRAC *equal* to the original LRAC. On the CRS portion of the LRAC, LRAC is always at a minimum.

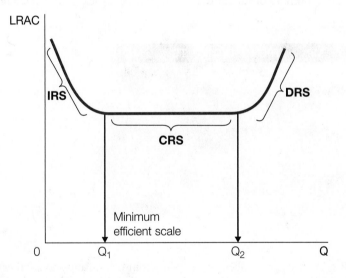

KEY TERMS

profit	long run
minimizing costs	variable inputs
positive economic profits	total product, TP
economic losses	marginal product, MP
normal economic profits	MP = ΔQ/Δ#of inputs
production function	diminishing marginal product
technically efficient technology	average product, AP
fixed inputs	AP = Q/#of inputs
short run	total fixed costs, TFC

average fixed costs, AFC

total variable costs, TVC

average variable costs, AVC

total cost

average total cost, ATC

marginal cost, MC

short-run cost structure

scale

long-run average cost curve, LRAC

efficient scale

increasing returns to scale, IRS

decreasing returns to scale, DRS

constant returns to scale, CRS

SOLVED EXAMPLE PROBLEMS

1. The Big Clean Company assembles central vacuum cleaning systems at a small plant in Welland. It pays each employee $19 per hour for a 7.5 hour day, that is, $142.50 per day. The company's only responsibility is to hire labour (everything else is provided by the manufacturer) and assemble, test, and pack the vacuum cleaners. There is a small fixed cost of $50 per day. Here is the production function for Big Clean; output is measured in number of vacuums assembled, tested, packaged, and ready to go out the door:

L	Q	MP	TFC	TVC	TC	MC
1	12					
2	30					
3	54					
4	84					
5	106					
6	123					
7	133					

Fill out the above table.

To find MP: MP = $\Delta Q/\Delta L$ (remember, we're going from one quantity to another)

When Q = 12, MP = $\Delta Q/\Delta L$ = 12/1 = 12

When Q = 30, MP = $\Delta Q/\Delta L$ = 18/1 = 18

When Q = 54, MP = $\Delta Q/\Delta L$ = 24/1 = 24

When Q = 84, MP = $\Delta Q/\Delta L$ = 30/1 = 30

When Q = 106, MP = $\Delta Q/\Delta L$ = 22/1 = 22

When Q = 123, MP = $\Delta Q/\Delta L$ = 17/1 = 17

When Q = 133, MP = $\Delta Q/\Delta L$ = 10/1 = 10

TFCs are fixed at the same amount no matter how much is being produced. The TFC value is $50 for every level of output.

TVCs are solely the company's labour costs (that's the only variable input). Simply multiply the number of workers by their daily wage, $142.50. Notice that more workers produce more output, so as output increases, TVCs increase (they're paying more workers).

For TC, just add TFC plus TVC.

Let's fill out the table with these values before we calculate MC.

L	Q	MP	TFC	TVC	TC	MC
1	12	12	50	142.5	192.5	
2	30	18	50	285	335	
3	54	24	50	427.5	477.5	
4	84	30	50	570	620	
5	106	22	50	712.5	762.5	
6	123	17	50	855	905	
7	133	10	50	997.5	1047.5	

To find MC: MC $= \Delta TC/\Delta Q$ (remember, we're going from one quantity to another)

When Q = 12, MC $= \Delta TC/\Delta Q = (192.50 - 50)/(12 - 0) = 142.50/12 = 11.88$

When Q = 30, MC $= \Delta TC/\Delta Q = 142.5/18 = 7.92$

When Q = 54, MC $= \Delta TC/\Delta Q = 142.5/24 = 5.94$

When Q = 84, MC $= \Delta TC/\Delta Q = 142.5/30 = 4.75$

When Q = 106, MC $= \Delta TC/\Delta Q = 142.5/22 = 6.48$

When Q = 123, MC $= \Delta TC/\Delta Q = 142.5/17 = 8.38$

When Q = 133, MC $= \Delta TC/\Delta Q = 142.5/10 = 14.25$

NOTICE: MC = wage/MP, just like we determined for Tom's Donut Hut.

Here's the complete table:

L	Q	MP	TFC	TVC	TC	MC
1	12	12	50	142.5	192.5	11.88
2	30	18	50	285	335	7.92
3	54	24	50	427.5	477.5	5.94
4	84	30	50	570	620	4.75
5	106	22	50	712.5	762.5	6.48
6	123	17	50	855	905	8.38
7	133	10	50	997.5	1047.5	14.25

NOTICE: MC is at a minimum when MP is at a maximum. MC increases as MP diminishes. Not a coincidence. We expected to see that.

2. The diagram below shows the long-run average cost curve for Coronation Clothiers, a manufacturer of fine ladies' coats. Owner Shelley is considering expansion in the next couple of years. Quantity is measured in number of coats completed per week.

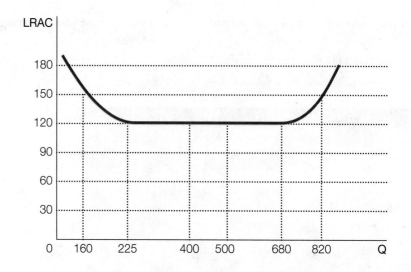

a) What quantity is the point of minimum efficient scale?

It's the smallest quantity of output the firm needs to produce to minimize LRAC. In this example, LRAC is first minimized at LRAC = $120, at Q = 225 coats.

b) Over what range does the firm experience constant returns to scale?

CRS means that LRAC do not change as output changes. In our example, there are CRS over the range of output from 225 to 680 coats.

c) At a level of output Q = 160, what type of returns to scale is the firm experiencing?

The firm can lower LRAC by increasing output, so the firm is experiencing increasing returns to scale.

d) At a level of output Q = 820, what type of returns to scale is the firm experiencing?

The firm can lower LRAC by decreasing output, so the firm is experiencing decreasing returns to scale.

PROBLEMS

1. The calculation of short-run costs is straightforward, mechanical and, well, boring. Fill in the following table for a firm's daily production plan and you're good to go.

L	Q	MP	TC	MC	TFC	AFC	TVC	AVC
1	25	25			90		600	
2	54	29						
3	95	41						
4	122	27						
5	144	22						
6	153	9						

2. A firm has a total cost function $TC = 258Q + 70$. Use this function to answer the following questions.

   a) What is the firm's total variable cost?

   b) What is the firm's total fixed cost?

c) What is the firm's average variable cost?

d) What is the firm's average fixed cost?

e) What is the firm's average total cost?

f) What is the firm's marginal cost?

SOLUTIONS

1.

L	Q	MP	TC	MC	TFC	AFC	TVC	AVC
1	25	25	690	24	90	3.6	600	24
2	54	29	1290	20.7	90	1.7	1200	22.22
3	95	41	1890	14.7	90	0.9	1800	18.95
4	122	27	2490	22.2	90	0.7	2400	19.67
5	144	22	3090	27.3	90	0.63	3000	20.83
6	153	9	3690	66.7	90	0.59	3600	23.53

2. A firm has a total cost function $TC = 258Q + 70$. Use this function to answer the following questions.

a) What is the firm's total variable cost?

$TVC = 258Q$ It's the part of TC based on Q.

b) What is the firm's total fixed cost?

$TFC = 70$ It's the constant in TC.

c) What is the firm's average variable cost?

$AVC = TVC/Q = 258Q/Q = 258$.

d) What is the firm's average fixed cost?

$AFC = TFC/Q = 70/Q$.

e) What is the firm's average total cost?

$ATC = TC/Q = 258 + 70/Q$ As well, $ATC = AVC + AFC$.

f) What is the firm's marginal cost?

$MC = 258$ For each additional unit of output produced, TC will increase by $258. MC is always the slope of the TC function.

CHAPTER 8

Perfect Competition

MAIN CONCEPTS AND DEFINITIONS

We defined perfect competition in Chapter 3, but let's briefly do it again so it's fresh.

Perfect Competition: a market structure typified by many small firms selling homogeneous output. Firms can enter or exit the industry freely. Consumers and firms are price takers; everyone knows that the market equilibrium price is the price that buyers will pay and that producers will receive for every good bought and sold. Think of the price of the good as given (determined by market forces).

In the last chapter we examined costs of production. Now we turn our attention to revenues.

Average Revenue, AR: the revenue generated by the sale of a typical unit of output. $AR = TR/Q$. Since $TR = P \star Q$, then $AR = (P \star Q)/Q = P$. That is, $AR = P$.

Marginal Revenue, MR is the addition to the firm's total revenue from the sale of another good. "If I produce and sell one more good, how much will my total revenue increase (or possibly decrease)?" Marginal revenue is the slope of the total revenue function. Total revenue is at a maximum when $MR = 0$. $MR = \Delta TR/\Delta Q$.

Since P is given in perfect competition, every additional good sold adds exactly the price the firm receives for it to its total revenue. Increase Q by one and you increase TR by P. This gives us an important relationship: in perfect competition, $P = MR$. <u>This is only true in perfect competition where everyone is a price taker.</u> And, since $AR = P$ and $MR = P$, then $AR = MR = P$.

Since we know about TR, TC and profit, we can draw the profit-maximizing picture:

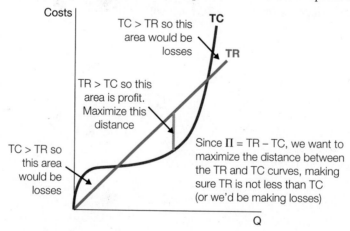

How does a firm decide how much to produce to maximize its profit? It decides using marginal thinking.

If producing an additional good would add more to total revenue than it would to total cost, the firm should produce that good—it makes a profit on it. This is saying that if MR > MC, produce that good. If, on the other hand, a firm notices that at the current quantity, the addition to total revenue of the last good produced is less than the addition to total cost, then the firm should cut back on production—it is making a loss. This is saying that if MR < MC, the firm should reduce output.

So, if MR > MC, increase output and if MR < MC, reduce output. Keep doing either, whichever one is warranted by the level of production, until you get to the point where if you produced one more good, it would add nothing to your profit or if you cut back by one good, that would do nothing to help your profit. This would be the case where MR = MC. Our profit-maximizing decision rule is:

A profit-maximizing firm will produce a quantity of output such that MR = MC.

But this is perfect competition where P = MR. Let's set MR = P in our profit-maximizing rule. Then, **a perfectly competitive firm will produce a quantity of output such that P = MC.**

- Setting MR = MC to maximize profit is true for any firm in any market structure.
- Setting P = MC to maximize profit is only true for a perfectly competitive firm where P is given.

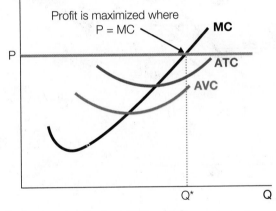

Producing at a level where MR ≠ MC:

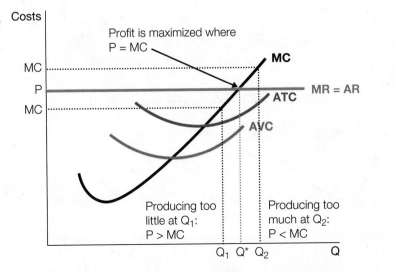

The firm will always choose its output level by setting P = MC. There's a clear relationship between price and quantity supplied by the firm. The firm's supply curve is its MC curve (not all of it; we'll explain that in a minute).

SHORT-RUN PROFITS AND LOSSES

We know that $\Pi = TR - TC$. Let's play with this equation without changing the equality.

Multiply the right hand side by 1 (we're preserving the identity) but let's use Q/Q (which equals 1). Then, $\Pi = (TR - TC) \star Q/Q$

$$= (TR/Q - TC/Q) \star Q$$
$$= (PQ/Q - TC/Q) \star Q$$
$$= (P - ATC) \star Q$$

We can now write profit as $\Pi = (P - ATC) \star Q$ where $P - ATC$ is the profit per unit. We can illustrate profit (and loss) on our SR cost diagram.

Positive Economic Profit: P > ATC

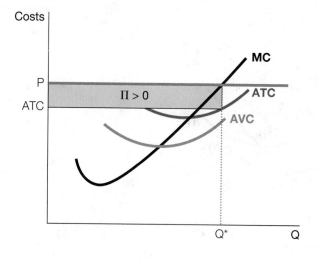

Economic Loss: P < ATC

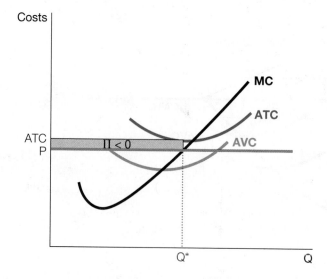

Zero (Normal) Economic Profit: P = minATC

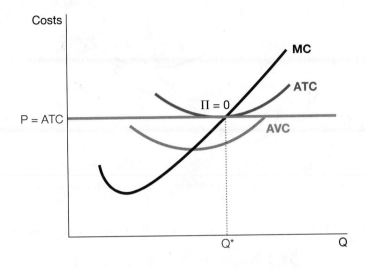

Don't forget—zero economic profit is just the expected, decent return for a firm in the market; you could be making a very nice accounting profit. The quantity produced when P = minATC is the **breakeven quantity**.

A FIRM'S SR SHUTDOWN DECISION

Sometimes things happen in a market that can temporarily impact firms. For example, lumber prices are stable throughout the housing construction season, but once winter arrives, the demand for lumber falls, as does its price. In spring, demand and price return to their higher level. What does a firm do if the winter lumber price falls so low that it is now losing money?

The firm has 2 choices: it can continue to produce and lose money until the price comes back up or it can temporarily shut down and wait for the price to come back up and then re-open.

If it decides to shut down temporarily, it still has to pay its fixed costs. The mortgage, bank loans, alarm system, heating bills (so the water pipes don't freeze and burst)—these bills have to be paid even if the firm doesn't produce anything. Where the firm saves is by not having to pay any variable costs. If they shut down, there are no labour costs, no raw material suppliers to be paid, and so on. The firm's loss, then, is equal to its fixed costs.

If the firm could cover its variable costs, it would be smart to stay open. Shutting down even for a very short time could mean a permanent loss of customers and revenue. In order to cover variable costs, the price has to be high enough so that what the firm receives as revenue for a good—the price—covers the variable cost of producing that good—its AVC. That is, keep producing in the SR as long as P > minimum AVC.

Here, P > AVC. Even though the firm is making a loss (since P < ATC) it can still pay its labour, materials' suppliers, and so on. And because P is greater than AVC, the difference P − AVC goes toward paying its fixed costs and thus reducing its losses.

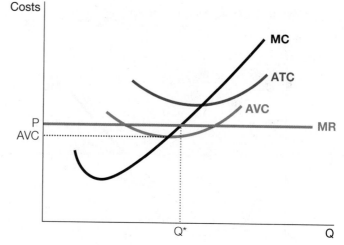

We now know exactly what the firm's SR supply curve looks like: it is the MC curve above minAVC, and 0 otherwise.

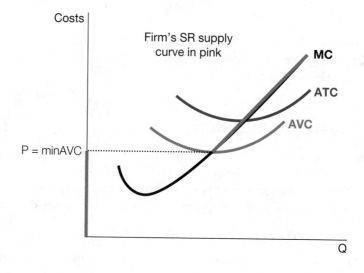

ENTRY AND EXIT IN THE LR

Losses occur when P < minATC. In the LR, firms making consistent losses will eventually leave the industry. This is called LR <u>exit</u>. Don't confuse exit with shutdown (shutdown is temporary and a SR concept).

When firms exit an industry because there are losses, the market supply curve shifts back and a new equilibrium with a higher price results. If the new price is still below minATC, more firms will exit. Exit will continue until supply has shifted back to the point where price has risen to equal minimum average total cost. At P = minATC, firms are no longer losing money; they are making normal economic profits and there is no longer any incentive for firms to exit. Exiting stops.

If firms in the industry are making consistent positive profits, there will be entry of new firms into the market. Positive profits are those atypical, crazy high profits that make an industry very attractive to entrepreneurs; these occur when P > minATC. The entry of new firms will shift the market supply curve to the right, resulting in a new equilibrium with a new, lower price. If the new price is still above minATC, entry of new firms will continue until the supply curve has shifted right to the point where price has fallen to equal minimum average total cost. At P = minATC, firms are no longer making crazy high profits; they are making normal economic profits and there is no longer any incentive for new firms to enter. Entry stops.

When there is no entry or exit in an industry, we say that the market is in **LR equilibrium**. LR equilibrium in a perfectly competitive market results when:

- P = MC in the SR (firms are maximizing SR profits)
- P = minATC in the SR (firms are making zero economic profits in the SR)
- P = minimum LRAC (firms must also be making zero economic profits in the LR so no firms think about entering or exiting down the road). This means that firms produce at efficient scale in the LR.

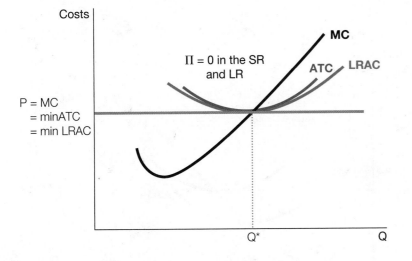

Example: How Firms Get to Equilibrium

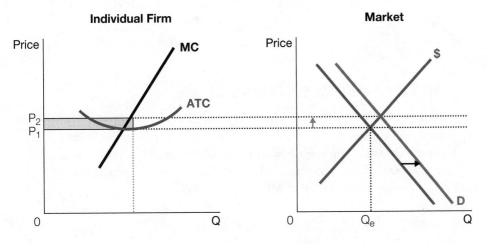

Suppose we start in LR equilibrium. An increase in demand increases market price. At P_2, firms are now making positive economic profits. New firms will enter the industry.

As firms enter, the supply curve shifts right and price falls. Entry will continue until the price returns to the original equilibrium price and firms are again making zero economic profits in LR equilibrium.

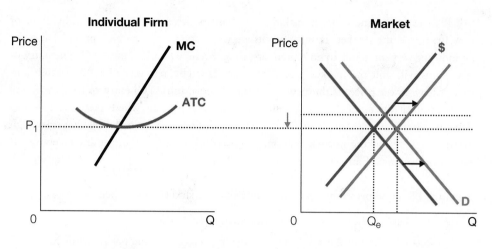

If firms exit the industry in the LR when P < minATC, we now know what the firm's LR supply curve looks like. It is the portion of the MC curve above minATC, and 0 otherwise.

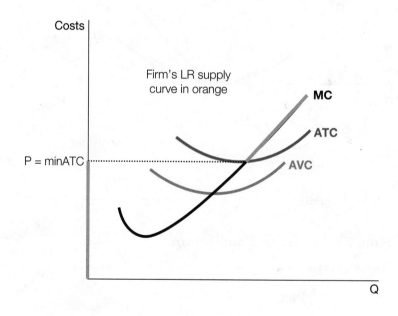

A COMPETITIVE FIRM'S DEMAND CURVE

Every firm knows that it will sell its good at the market equilibrium price. If a firm tried to charge a higher price, no one would buy from it; they could buy the identical good at the lower market price from one of many, many other firms. Thus, the demand faced by the <u>firm</u> is perfectly elastic. It is a horizontal line where P = market equilibrium price. So, for a perfectly competitive firm, P = MR = AR = D.

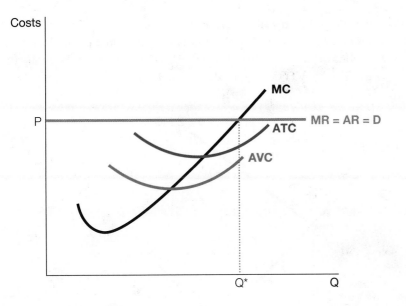

SR MARKET SUPPLY

We know that an individual firm's SR supply curve is its MC curve above minAVC. To get the market supply curve, we add up all the individual firms' supplies = we add up all their MC curves. Now we can think of the market supply curve as one big aggregate MC curve such that market S = ΣMC of all individual firms. That's why, for example, we use the market supply curve to reflect firms' costs when we compute producer surplus.

LR MARKET SUPPLY

If the industry is a **constant cost industry**, firms' average and marginal costs of production do not change when the quantity produced changes. They will always be happy to supply at the same price which will be equal to their minimum LRAC in equilibrium. The LR market supply curve will be a horizontal line at P = min LRAC.

If the industry is an **increasing cost industry**, the more output firms produce, the higher their average and marginal costs of production. They'll need to receive a higher price for their output in order to cover these higher costs. The LR market supply curve will be upward sloping.

PRODUCER SURPLUS AND PROFITS

When firms have fixed costs, producer surplus and firm profits are not the same. Why bring this up now? Because we have just learned that the market supply curve is the big aggregate MC curve for the industry. MC measures the addition to TC as Q increases. This is a change in variable costs because fixed costs don't change when Q changes; then, MC is an addition to TVC. So, the area under the MC curve must be total variable costs.

Profit is Π = TR − TC
= TR − (TVC + TFC)
= TR − TVC − TFC

Let's draw TR. TR = PQ, the area of the rectangle outlined in purple, below. TVC, as explained above, is the area in green. PS is the dark blue triangle. You can see that, visually, PS = TR − TVC. But we just noted that ∏ = TR − TVC − TFC, and substituting PS for TR -TVC, we get ∏ = PS − TFC. That is, **PS = ∏ + TFC.**

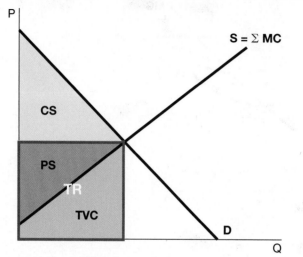

THE ALGEBRA OF PERFECT COMPETITION

Recall that whatever market equilibrium price is, that is the price that firms know they will sell their output for. Marginal revenue equals price in perfect competition, and since profit is maximized where marginal revenue equals marginal cost, that means price equals marginal cost for competitive firms. They take the market price, equate it to their marginal cost, and determine how much they will produce. We've done that diagrammatically, so now let's use equations.

EXAMPLE

Market demand is P = 1020 − Q. Market supply is P = 0.02Q. A firm has MC = 2Q.

First, you have to find market price. **You can't do anything if you don't have market price.**

$$1020 − Q = 0.02Q$$
$$1020 = 1.02Q$$
$$Q = 1000$$
$$P = 1020 − 1000 = \$20$$

Now set market P = MC = 20: 20 = 2Q
$$Q = 10$$

Our firm will produce 10 units of output and sell it for $20 per unit for total revenue TR = $200.

Now suppose that the firm's ATC = Q + 10/Q. ATC when Q = 10 is ATC = 10 + 10/10 = $11. Since profit = (P − ATC)Q, this firm's profit is ∏ = (20 − 11)10 = $90.

The firm is making positive economic profit. If this is a representative firm, then the supranormal profits in the industry will attract entry in the long run. This will shift the market supply to the right, price will be driven down, and eventually price will reach minimum ATC. Firms will then be earning zero, normal economic profits, and entry will stop. The market will reach a long-run equilibrium.

In long-run equilibrium, price will equal minimum ATC (which will equal minimum LRAC). For this firm, suppose we are told that ATC is at a minimum at $6.32. *Note to calculus lovers—to find minimum ATC, take the derivative of ATC with respect to Q and set it equal to 0. You'll get Q = 3.16 so that ATC = 6.32 at its minimum. Since this is an introductory course, you are not expected to use calculus and will always be told the value of minimum ATC where required.*

Long-run price is therefore P = 6.32. We know the supply curve shifted when new firms entered, but we don't know the new equation. But, we do know the equation of the demand curve. If we substitute P = 6.32 into our demand curve, quantity demanded in the long run will be:

6.32 = 1020 − Q

Q = 1013.68 (which will be equilibrium Q traded)

If P = 6.32, set MC = 6.32 to see how much each firm will produce in the long run:

6.32 = 20Q

Q = 3.16

If each firm produces Q = 3.16 and Q_d = 1013.68, there will be 1013.68/3.16 = 320.79 firms in the long run in equilibrium (yes, you can round this number and say there's about 321 firms in the industry).

Here's what the whole deal looks like:

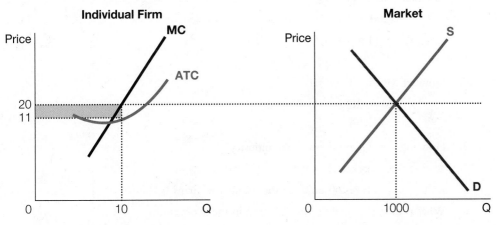

At the initial market equilibrium price, firms were earning positive economic profits.

New firms entered the market, drove market price down to equal minimum ATC = min LRAC, and long-run equilibrium resulted.

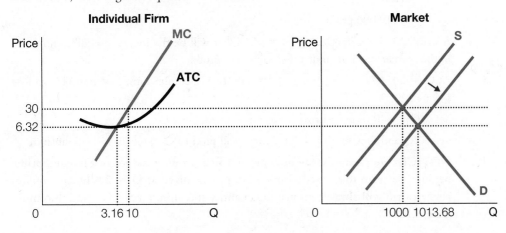

perfect competition
average revenue, AR
Marginal Revenue, MR
breakeven quantity

LR equilibrium
constant cost industry
increasing cost industry

SOLVED EXAMPLE PROBLEMS

In a perfectly competitive market, market demand is given by $Q_d = 1200 - P$ and market supply is given by $Q_s = 9P$. A typical firm has $MC = 2Q$ and $ATC = Q + 400/Q$.

1. How much will a typical firm produce to maximize profit?

    A firm will set $P = MC$, so we need to find market equilibrium price before we do anything else.

    In equilibrium, $Q_d = Q_s$

    $$1200 - P = 9P$$
    $$1200 = 10P$$
    $$P = 120$$

    Now set $MC = 120$:

    $$120 = 2Q$$
    $$Q = 60$$

2. How many firms are there in the industry?

    At $P = 120$, market $Q = 9 \star 120 = 1080$.

    Each firm produces 60 units, so the number of firms is $1080/60 = 18$ firms.

3. What is the profit or loss for each firm in the short run?

    $$ATC = 60 + 400/60 = 66.67$$
    $$Profit = (P - ATC)Q$$
    $$= (120 - 66.67) \star 60$$
    $$= \$3199.80 \text{ profit}$$

4. A firm's ATC is minimized at $Q = 20$. What will be the long-run equilibrium price in the market and how much will each firm produce?

    At $Q = 20$, $ATC = 20 + 400/20 = \$40$. In LR equilibrium, $P = minATC$ so $P = \$40$ in the LR.

    Set $MC = \$40$ to get a firm's output in LR equilibrium:

    $40 = 2Q$ and therefore $Q = 20$. A firm will produce 20 units in LR equilibrium.

    NOTICE: We already knew how much a firm would produce in LR equilibrium because we were told that a firm's ATC is minimized at $Q = 20$. In LR equilibrium, a firm will always produce the quantity that minimizes ATC (and thus minimizes LRAC).

5. How many firms will there be in the long run?

Substitute the LR price of $40 into the demand curve to solve for Q:

$Q_d = 1200 - 40 = 1160$

Each firm produces 20 so the total number of firms will be $1160/20 = 58$ firms in the LR.

6. Sketch a diagram of LR equilibrium in this market.

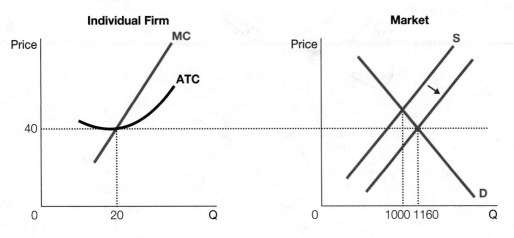

1. The following diagram illustrates a perfectly competitive firm's SR cost structure:

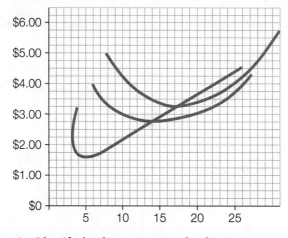

a) Identify the three curves on the diagram.

b) Suppose the market price is $4.00. Illustrate the firm's profit-maximizing level of output and calculate and illustrate its profit or loss.

c) What is the firm's breakeven price and quantity?

d) What is the firm's shutdown price?

2. A typical perfectly competitive firm faces market demand and supply given by Q_d = 1000 − 10P and Q_s = 40P. The firm has MC = Q and ATC = 0.5Q + 20/Q. The firm's total cost is TC = $0.5Q^2$ + 20.

a) How much will the firm produce to maximize profit?

b) What is the profit or loss for the firm in the short run?

c) How many firms are there in the industry?

d) A firm's ATC is minimized at Q = 6.32. What will be the long-run equilibrium price in the market and how much will each firm produce?

e) In the SR, what is the price elasticity of the *firm's* demand?

f) What is the value of the firm's short-run TVC? TFC? AVC? AFC?

g) Assume that this is a constant cost industry. What is the equation of the long-run market supply curve?

1. The following diagram illustrates a perfectly competitive firm's SR cost structure:

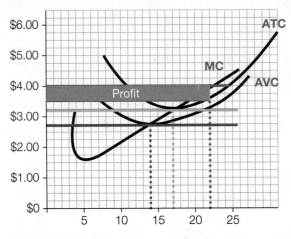

a) Identify the three curves on the diagram.

On the diagram.

b) Suppose the market price is $4.00. Illustrate the firm's profit-maximizing level of output and calculate and illustrate its profit or loss.

$\Pi = (P - ATC)Q.$

$= (4 - 3.50)22$

$= \$11.00$

c) What is the firm's breakeven price and quantity?

Breakeven at P = minATC: where P = 3.25 and Q = 17 (the green lines).

d) What is the firm's shutdown price?

Shutdown at P = minAVC: where P = 2.75 and Q = 14.

Remember, this would be a temporary shutdown.

2. A typical perfectly competitive firm faces market demand and supply given by $Q_d = 1000 - 10P$ and $Q_s = 40P$. The firm has MC = Q and ATC = 0.5Q + 20/Q. The firm's total cost is $TC = 0.5Q^2 + 20$.

a) How much will the firm produce to maximize profit?

Find market equilibrium price first. Set $Q_d = Q_s$:

$1000 - 10P = 40P$

$1000 = 50P$

$P = 20$

Set P = MC for the firm:

$20 = Q$

The firm will produce 20 units of output to maximize its profit.

b) What is the profit or loss for the firm in the short run?

$\Pi = (P - ATC)Q$ or $\Pi = TR - TC$. Pick whichever equation you'd like to use.

ATC when Q = 20 is ATC = 0.5(20) + 20/20 = 11

$\prod = (P - ATC)Q = (20 - 11)20 = \$180$

Or, $TR = 20(20) = 400$ and $TC = 0.5(20^2) + 20 = 220$

$\prod = 400 - 220 = \$180$

c) How many firms are there in the industry?

At $P = 20$, market $Q = 800$. If each firm is producing 20 units, the number of firms in the market is $800/20 = 40$

d) A firm's ATC is minimized at $Q = 6.32$. What will be the long-run equilibrium price in the market and how much will each firm produce?

At $Q = 6.32$, $minATC = 0.5(6.32) + 20/6.32 = 6.32 = LR$ price

Each firm will produce the ATC-minimizing quantity which we are told is 6.32.

Alternatively, set $P = MC$: $P = Q$ so $6.32 = Q$

e) In the SR, what is the price elasticity of the *firm's* demand?

The firm's demand curve is the price it faces, so demand is perfectly horizontal and therefore elasticity => infinity.

f) What is the value of the firm's short-run TVC? TFC?

TVC is the part of TC that has a Q in it:

$TVC = 0.5Q^2 = 0.5(20^2) = \$200$

TFC is the part of TC that is a constant:

$TFC = 20$

$AVC = TVC/Q = 200/20 = \$10$

$AFC = TFC/Q = 20/20 = \$1$

g) Assume that this is a constant cost industry. What is the equation of the long-run market supply curve?

LR S will be horizontal at $P = min\ LRAC = minATC = \$6.32$.

CHAPTER 9
Monopoly

MAIN CONCEPTS AND DEFINITIONS

A **monopoly** is a single seller of a good or service for which there is no close substitute. Since it is the only firm in the market, it sets its own price. It has to serve the entire market so the market demand curve is also the firm's demand curve.

A monopoly maximizes profit by choosing a level of output such that MR = MC. In perfect competition, firms set P = MC because P = MR. In monopoly, P > MR. Because the monopolist has a downward-sloping demand curve, in order to sell more goods, it has to lower its price on <u>all</u> the goods it sells. This example will help you:

EXAMPLE

The GB Estates Winery sells wine by the 750ml bottle. The table reports GB's demand schedule and revenues.

Q	P	TR = PQ	AR = TR/Q	MR = ΔTR/ΔQ
1	40	40	40	
2	35	70	35	30
3	30	90	30	20
4	25	100	25	10
5	20	100	20	0
6	15	90	15	−10
7	10	70	10	−20
8	5	40	5	−30

Notice: AR = P (it always does), but MR < P. Why? GB can sell one bottle of wine at a price of $40. If it wants to sell 2, it has to lower the price from $40 to $35 (downward-sloping demand curve). The addition of the second bottle doesn't add $35 to TR because the price of the first bottle had to drop by $5 in order for GB to sell *both* bottles. So price is $35 per bottle but the MR from the second bottle is only $30.

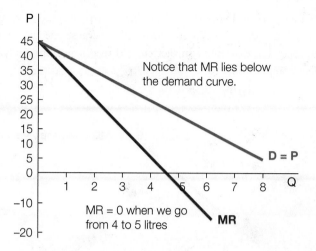

The monopoly maximizes profit by setting its MR = MC and choosing Q. It then goes up to the demand curve to see the maximum price it can charge for that quantity of output.

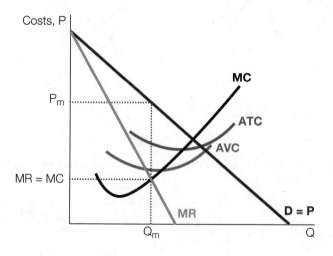

Profit for any firm is $\Pi = (P - ATC)Q$.

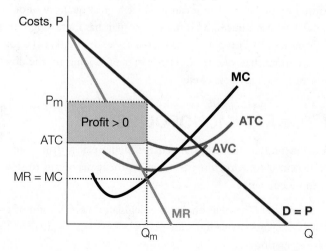

A monopoly charges a higher price and produces less output compared to the perfectly competitive outcome. The result is a **deadweight loss** in surplus because the market is served by one firm which produces <u>less</u> than many smaller competitive firms; monopoly is inefficient compared to perfect competition.

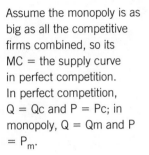

Assume the monopoly is as big as all the competitive firms combined, so its MC = the supply curve in perfect competition. In perfect competition, Q = Qc and P = Pc; in monopoly, Q = Qm and P = P_m.

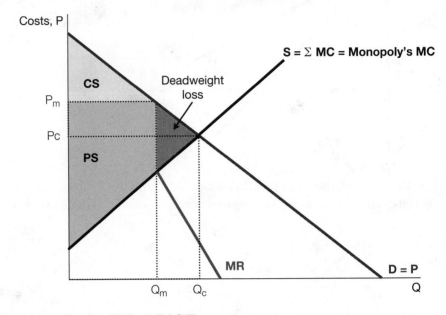

HOW MONOPOLIES ARISE

Monopolies exist because there are barriers to entry of rival firms in the market:

- A firm may own a key resource required to make its good and no other firm can acquire it.

- A firm may have a patent that gives it the sole right to produce its good or the government gives it monopoly rights in a specific market.

- A firm may conduct its affairs with the goal of being a monopoly and be successful.

- A firm may be a natural monopoly where it can produce a great quantity of output and its ATC drops the *more* it produces. This means the firm has increasing returns to scale over a significant range of output and can serve the entire market at a lower ATC than if there were more than one firm. The firm is producing on the downward sloping portion of its average cost curve.

PUBLIC POLICY TOWARD MONOPOLIES

Monopolies are inefficient. They produce too little and charge higher prices than would be found in the competitive outcome. Not surprisingly, the government may want to step in and try to correct some of the inefficiency.

- In Canada we have the federal Competition Act that legislates with the aim of preventing anti-competitive business behaviour (for example, laws against mergers that would severely limit competition).

- The government may regulate the monopoly to keep the firm's profits in line with the fair returns earned by competitive firms. It could make the monopoly charge a price of P = MC or P = ATC. Forcing the latter may still result in an inefficient level of output but at least the monopoly is not making supranormal profit (which consumers don't like).

Example: Regulating that the monopoly charge P = ATC:

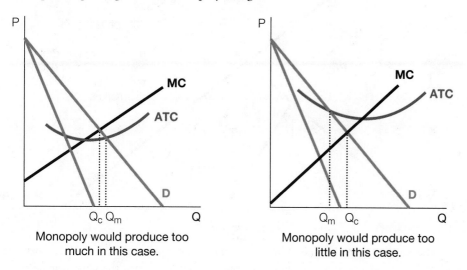

Monopoly would produce too much in this case.

Monopoly would produce too little in this case.

- The government could just run the monopoly itself (Crown Corporations in Canada). Examples are the CBC and Canada Post at the federal level and the Beer Store in some provinces.

- If the inefficiency is small the government may just stay out of it.

PRICE DISCRIMINATION

Price discrimination: charging different prices to different customers even though the cost of producing the goods is the same.

In order to be able to price discriminate the firm has to 1) be able to segment the market and 2) be able to set its own prices (so that eliminates perfectly competitive firms).

THREE KINDS OF PRICE DISCRIMINATION

First-Degree Price Discrimination: also called perfect price discrimination. A firm charges a different price to each customer based on each consumer's willingness to pay (reservation price). In this model, the firm has to know each customer's reservation price, which is hard to do in practice. Example: an accountant charges each client a different price.

The firm doesn't just produce where MR = MC. Because it can charge different prices, it can produce more and keep charging a P > MC up to the point where it produces the competitive quantity. As long as it can get a P > MC, it is making a profit on each additional unit sold and will keep producing. Under perfect price discrimination, P = MR and there is no deadweight loss in surplus. However, there is no consumer surplus; every customer pays an amount exactly equal to their willingness to pay, so they receive no benefit and the firm appropriates all of the surplus in the market for itself.

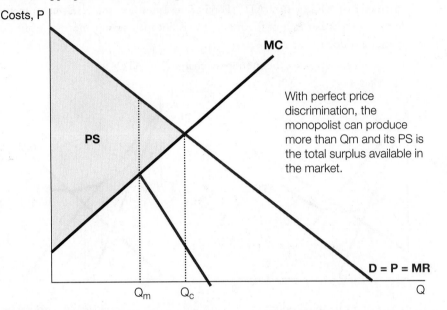

With perfect price discrimination, the monopolist can produce more than Q_m and its PS is the total surplus available in the market.

Second-Degree Price Discrimination: The price that consumers pay varies according to the quantity they purchase, but all consumers face the same pricing scheme. An example is a BOGO sale (buy one, get one half off).

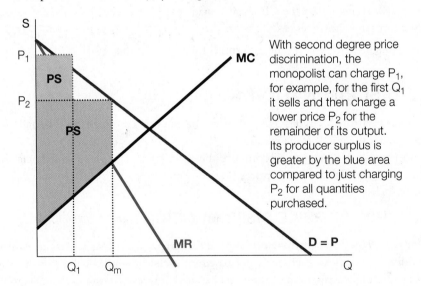

With second degree price discrimination, the monopolist can charge P_1, for example, for the first Q_1 it sells and then charge a lower price P_2 for the remainder of its output. Its producer surplus is greater by the blue area compared to just charging P_2 for all quantities purchased.

Third-Degree Price Discrimination: also called ordinary price discrimination. The firm charges different prices to different groups of consumers; everyone in the same group pays the same price. Example: women pay more for a haircut than do men.

The firm chooses output by aggregating the MR curves from its different markets into one big MR. It sets that MR = MC and chooses total output Q. It then allocates that output in each market by setting each market MR = aggregate MR = MC. Then it gets the price in each market from each market's demand curve.

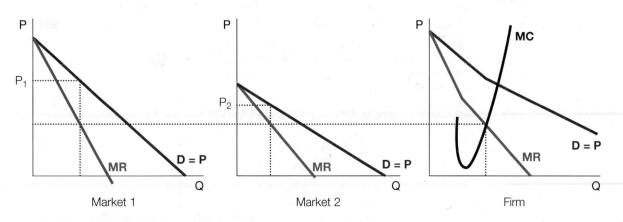

Market 1   Market 2   Firm

MONOPOLY SUPPLY CURVE

A monopoly **doesn't** have a supply curve. You can't ask a monopolist, "If price is such-and-such, how much will you produce?" The monopolist will tell you, "I set MR = MC, pick my output level, and THEN I choose price based on market demand." There is no clear relationship between P and Q for a monopolist like there is for a perfectly competitive firm which sets P = MC to decide Q.

KEY TERMS

monopoly	**first-degree price discrimination**
deadweight loss	**second-degree price discrimination**
price discrimination	**third-degree price discrimination**

SOLVED EXAMPLE PROBLEMS

A monopolist maximizes profit by finding the quantity at which marginal revenue equals marginal cost. But marginal revenue is not equal to price in any market but perfect competition (monopoly MR < P), so we need to know the equations for MR and MC. These equations will always be given to you in an introductory course.

A monopolist faces market demand of $P = 200 - Q$. Its $MR = 200 - 2Q$ and $MC = 2Q$. $ATC = Q$.

The firm sets MR = MC:

$$200 - 2Q = 2Q$$
$$200 = 4Q$$
$$Q = 50$$

To get price, substitute $Q = 50$ into the <u>demand</u> curve:

$$P = 200 - 50 = 150$$

ATC when $Q = 50$ is $ATC = 50$
The firm's profit is:

$$\text{Profit} = (P - ATC)Q$$
$$= (150 - 50) \star 50$$
$$= \$5000$$

Because a monopoly produces a lower quantity of output compared to the perfectly competitive outcome, there will be a deadweight loss in total surplus due to monopoly. Let's calculate it for our example. This is what our solution looks like diagrammatically so far:

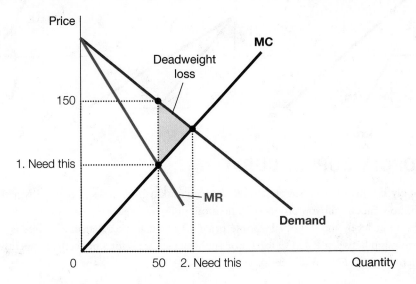

To get #1, substitute Q = 50 into either the MR or MC equation (let's use the MC equation).

MC = 2Q
MC = 2(50)
MC = 100

To get #2, set demand equal to marginal cost:

200 – Q = 2Q
200 = 3Q
Q = 66.67

Now we can fill in the missing values on our diagram:

The base of our triangle = 150 – 100 = 50

The height of our triangle = 66.67 – 50 = 16.67

DWL = 1/2(50)(16.67) = $416.75

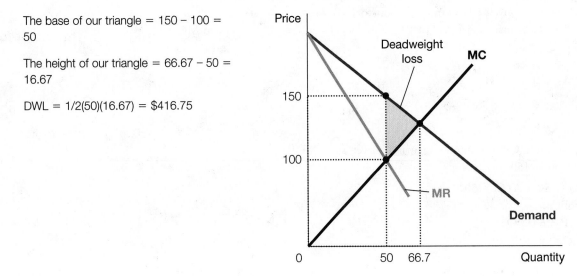

1. Front Publishing is the only printer of economics textbooks in town. They face a market demand of $P = 200 - 2Q$ for textbooks. Front's $MR = 200 - 4Q$. Their $TC = 2Q^2$, $MC = 4Q$, and their $ATC = 2Q$.

   Use the diagram below to add the sketches of your answers for the following questions.

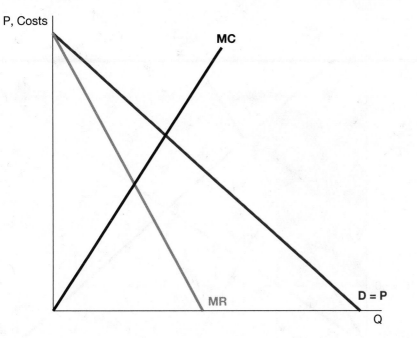

   a) What is Front's profit-maximizing level of output, selling price, and total profit? Illustrate these on the above diagram.

   b) What is deadweight loss in welfare due to the monopoly? Add this diagram to your diagram above.

   c) What is the monopoly's producer surplus? Illustrate this on your diagram.

1. Front Publishing is the only printer of economics textbooks in town. They face a market demand of $P = 200 - 2Q$ for textbooks. Front's $MR = 200 - 4Q$. Their $MC = 4Q$ and their $ATC = 2Q$.

   Use the diagram below to add the sketches of your answers for the following questions.

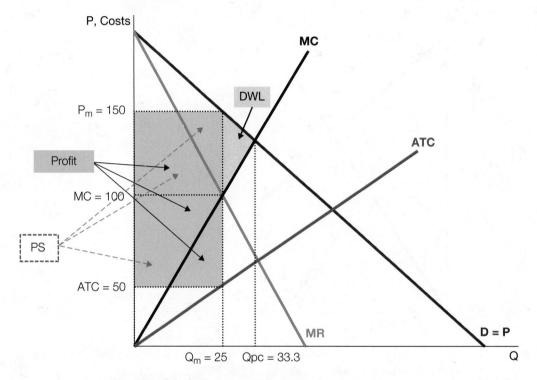

   a) What is Front's profit maximizing level of output, selling price, and total profit? Illustrate these on the above diagram.

   Set MR = MC: $200 - 4Q = 4Q$

   $8Q = 200$

   $Q = 25$

   Substitute Q = 25 into the <u>demand</u> curve to get P: $P = 200 - 2(25)$

   $P = \$150$

   $ATC = 2Q = 2(25) = \$50$ ATC is a linear ray through the origin.

   $\Pi = (P - ATC)Q = (150 - 50)25 = \$2500$ It's the area of the green rectangle.

   b) What is deadweight loss in welfare due to the monopoly? Add this diagram to your diagram above.

   First draw the DWL triangle so you know what values you need to find its area. You need the Q produced in a perfectly competitive market, so set P = MC which means setting D = MC since the demand curve is our price curve:

   $200 - 2Q = 4Q$

   $6Q = 200$

   $Q = 33.3$

You need the base length of the triangle, so you need the value for MC (or MR) at Q = 25:

MC = 4Q = 4(25) = 100   The base of the triangle = 150 – 100 = 50

DWL = 0.5(50)(33.3 – 25) = $207.50

c) What is the monopoly's producer surplus? Illustrate this on your diagram.

PS is the area under the price the firm receives above MC given that the firm produces 25 units of output. It's the area of the trapezoid drawn in dashed blue lines on the diagram:

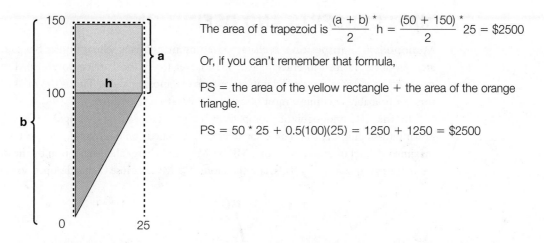

The area of a trapezoid is $\dfrac{(a + b)}{2} * h = \dfrac{(50 + 150)}{2} * 25 = \$2500$

Or, if you can't remember that formula,

PS = the area of the yellow rectangle + the area of the orange triangle.

PS = 50 * 25 + 0.5(100)(25) = 1250 + 1250 = $2500

NOTICE: In this example, PS was the same as profit. That's because there are no fixed costs. If there were fixed costs, PS = Π + TFC.

CHAPTER 10
Monopolistic Competition

MAIN CONCEPTS AND DEFINITIONS

Monopolistic competition is characterized by many firms selling similar but differentiated products. Firms can enter or exit the market freely (no barriers to entry). Firms are
price setters to some degree. Examples: restaurants, most retailers. This is the market structure we probably encounter most often in our day-to-day dealings.

In the SR, monopolistic competitors behave just like a monopoly. They have a
downward-sloping demand curve for their differentiated (unique) good, choose the profit-
maximizing level of output such that MR = MC, and charge the price given by the demand
curve for that quantity. P > MR and therefore P > MC because demand slopes downward.

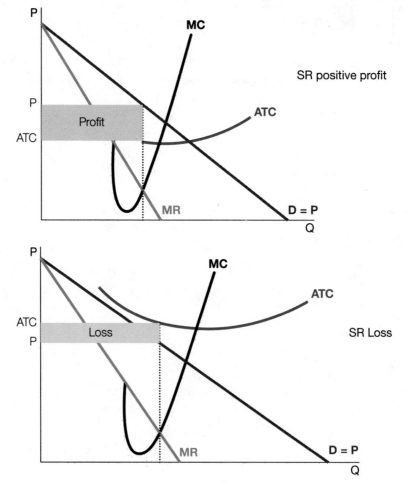

In the LR, firms behave just like perfect competition. Entry (when there are positive profits) or exit (when there are losses) will drive profits to zero economic profits at P = ATC (MR = MC at this point as well).

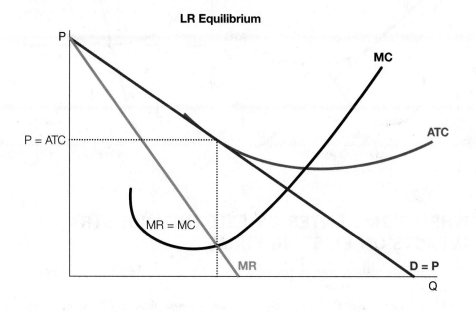

LR Equilibrium

In LR equilibrium:

The ATC curve is just tangent to the demand curve in LR equilibrium.

We can't be tangent at minATC like we are in perfect competition because the demand curve is downward sloping.

In the SR and even in LR equilibrium, there is a deadweight loss in surplus. The monopolistically competitive firm produces less than the socially efficient perfectly competitive outcome.

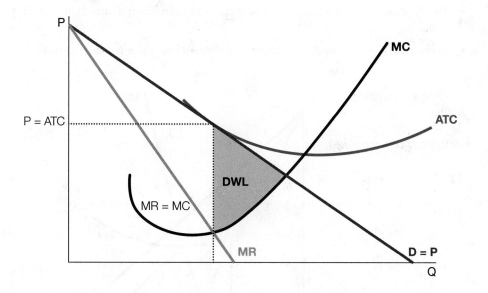

The monopolistically competitive firm has the ability to produce more Q (**excess capacity**) and lower its ATC. However, it would be making a loss because its ATC would be greater than the price it could get for that quantity.

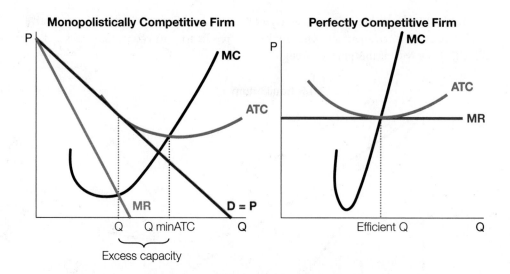

Monopolistically Competitive Firm

P

MC

ATC

MR

D = P

Q   Q minATC   Q

Excess capacity

Perfectly Competitive Firm

P

MC

ATC

MR

Efficient Q   Q

WHEN FIRMS ENTER OR EXIT THE INDUSTRY: IMPACTS ON EXISTING FIRMS

When firms are making positive economic profits, we know there will be entry of new firms.

Consider the market for fast-food restaurants. A new firm, Biddle Burgers, sets up shop in town:

- More burgers, fries, shakes, and desserts are available to consumers.

- There will be consumers who really like Biddle Burgers and now will only go there. This reduces the demand for the restaurants that were already there.

- The decrease in demand faced by the original firms means their demand curves shift to the left.

- Because the demand for the existing firms' burgers falls, there is a decline in their profits.

When new firms enter, existing firms' profits decrease (from green rectangle to blue rectangle).

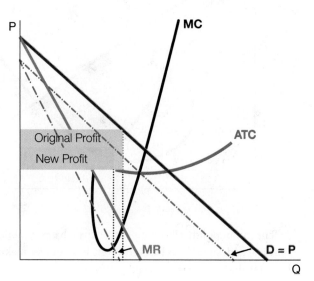

P

MC

ATC

Original Profit

New Profit

MR

D = P

Q

When firms are making losses, we know firms will leave the industry.

Honey's Hamburgers is one firm which can't compete, and after consistently losing money for months, it closes its doors and leaves the market.

- Now there are fewer fast-food choices offered to consumers.
- Honey's old customers will seek out the remaining restaurants for fast food, and the demand faced by the remaining firms will increase.
- The increase in demand will shift the remaining firms' demand curves to the right.
- The increase in demand will decrease any losses other firms were incurring.

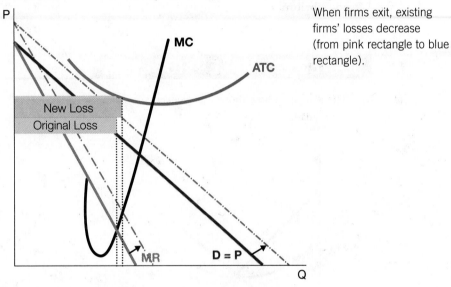

When firms exit, existing firms' losses decrease (from pink rectangle to blue rectangle).

ADVERTISING

Because monopolistic competitors want to differentiate their products, it's no surprise that often they are heavy advertisers. Think of all the ads you see for the numerous fast-food restaurants, clothing stores, and beauty products you encounter everywhere. Whether advertising is a good thing or bad depends on who you ask.

Good things said about advertising:

- It provides information to consumers about new products and services, sales, and so forth.
- It encourages price competition ("We'll match any competitor's price—just bring us their flyer").
- It allows new firms to enter an industry (they can advertise to make their presence and products known to consumers).
- It signals consumers that the product is of high quality (the firm wouldn't spend so much money to advertise a junk good because it wants repeat customers).

Bad things said about advertising:

- It could be a barrier to entry by helping existing firms build intense brand loyalty (a new firm wouldn't stand a chance of being competitive against a firm with a committed consumer base).

- It could increase prices by increasing the costs of production.
- It manipulates consumers into buying stuff they don't really want.
- When aimed at children, advertising is exploitative.

KEY TERMS

monopolistic competition   **excess capacity**
LR equilibrium

SOLVED EXAMPLE PROBLEMS

1. The diagram below shows the weekend demand for Chicken City's 10-piece bucket of Louisiana fried chicken:

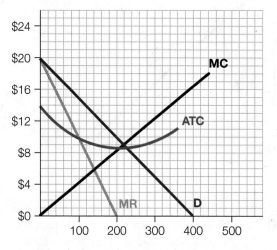

a) What is the profit-maximizing level of output, price and profit for Chicken City?

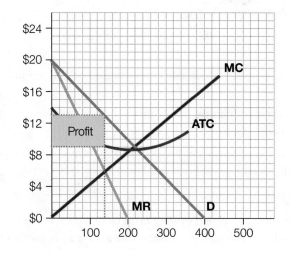

b) Suppose new firms enter the fast-food industry. Chicken City loses some of its customers to the competition and the demand curve shifts left as shown below:

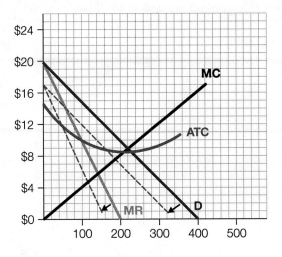

c) What are Chicken City's new quantity, price, and profit?

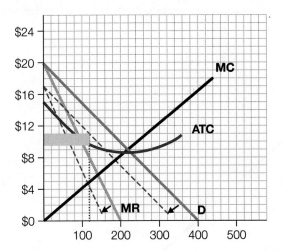

Set the new MR = MC, then go up to the new demand curve to get the price.

Q = 120 and P = $11.
ATC = $9.50
Π = (P − ATC)Q
   = (11 − 10)(120)
   = $180, less than profit before new firms entered.

1. The Econotrip travel agency sells weekend packages to Las Vegas. Its monthly demand is $P = 900 - Q$ and its $MR = 900 - 2Q$. It has $TC = 2Q^2$ with $MC = 4Q$ and $ATC = 2Q$ (ATC is linear in this example).

   a) What is the firm's monthly profit-maximizing number of travel packages, price, and profit?

   b) Suppose new travel agents open up for business. Econotrip sees its demand fall to $P = 600 - P$ with $MR = 600 - 2P$. What is Econotrip's new profit-maximizing number of travel packages, price, and profit?

   c) Sketch Econtrip's profit-maximizing outcome both before and after new travel agents entered the industry.

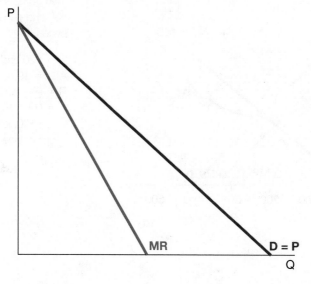

   d) What could Econotrip do to get its demand back up to where it was?

1. The Econotrip travel agency sells weekend packages to Las Vegas. Its monthly demand is $P = 900 - Q$ and its $MR = 900 - 2Q$. It has $TC = 2Q^2$ with $MC = 4Q$ and $ATC = 2Q$ (ATC is linear in this example).

    a) What is the firm's monthly profit maximizing number of travel packages, price, and profit?

        Set MR = MC, then go up to the demand curve to get the price.

        $900 - 2Q = 4Q$

        $6Q = 900$

        $Q = 150$ and $P = \$750$

        $ATC = \$300$

        $P = (P - ATC)Q$

        $\quad = (750 - 300)(150)$

        $\quad = \$67\ 500$

    b) Suppose new travel agents open up for business. Econotrip sees its demand fall to $P = 600 - Q$ with $MR = 600 - 2Q$. What is Econotrip's new profit-maximizing number of travel packages, price, and profit?

        Set the new MR = MC, then go up to the new demand curve to get the price.

        $600 - 2Q = 4Q$

        $6Q = 600$

        $Q = 100$ and $P = \$500$

        $ATC = \$200$

        $P = (P - ATC)Q$

        $\quad = (500 - 200)(100)$

        $\quad = \$30\ 000$

    c) Sketch Econtrip's profit-maximizing outcome both before and after new travel agents entered the industry.

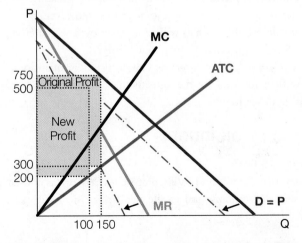

    d) What could Econotrip do to get its demand back up to where it was?

        It could advertise! Keep in mind that the money it spends on advertising would add to its costs so its SR cost structure would change.

CHAPTER 11

Oligopoly

MAIN CONCEPTS AND DEFINITIONS

Oligopoly is characterized by only a few, usually big firms selling homogeneous products. These firms are interdependent: the actions of one firm affects the profits of the others. Examples: sugar industry, soft drinks, big oil companies, and tobacco companies.

Like monopolies, we see barriers to entry in oligopolistic markets. If firms could enter freely to capitalize on positive economic profits, eventually the market would look like a perfectly competitive market. We'd see many firms all producing identical goods. Entry would drive the price down to approach MC and the quantity would approach the competitive equilibrium quantity. Firms would see their profits go to zero economic profits in the LR. Not surprisingly, oligopolistic firms want to limit entry into their industry so they can preserve their market shares and maintain positive economic profits.

There are some natural barriers to entry into an oligopoly. The set-up costs could be prohibitively high and successfully deter entry. Firms might behave in such a way that new firms would not be able to compete; existing firms could produce more than their profit-maximizing output level in order to flood the market and sell cheap.

Although illegal in most industrialized countries, sometimes firms will act co-operatively and collude to fix prices or market output levels. Colluding firms form a **cartel**, the best known of which is OPEC.[1] If firms manage to co-operate, it's generally *tacit* collusion so any dealings can't be traced.

More often than not, collusive agreements among firms are hard to maintain. Collusion requires firms to think in terms of joint action and joint profits. However, we know that firms (and anyone who is economically rational) will act in their own self-interest. Firm X is concerned about Firm X's profits; it doesn't care about Firm Y.

Even if firms did come to some kind of agreement about prices or quantity of output, there is temptation for any firm to cheat on the agreement and increase its profit at the expense of the other firms. Let's see how this works:

EXAMPLE: A VEGETABLE OIL DUOPOLY

A **duopoly** is a market with two firms.

Suppose every Saturday that Robin and Wills prepare barrels of their own pressed vegetable oil which they sell to restaurants and to the public. For simplicity assume that

---

[1] According to OPEC's website: "OPEC's objective is to co-ordinate and unify petroleum policies among Member Countries, in order to secure fair and stable prices for petroleum producers; an efficient, economic and regular supply of petroleum to consuming nations; and a fair return on capital to those investing in the industry." OPEC considers itself an intergovernmental organization. www.opec.org/opec web/en/about us/24.htm on November 11, 2014.

there are no production costs; TC = 0 and MC = 0. Robin and Wills know the demand schedule for vegetable oil:

Quantity	Price	TR
100	0	0
90	10	900
80	20	1600
70	30	2100
60	40	2400
50	50	2500
40	60	2400
30	70	2100
20	80	1600
10	90	900

Since there are no costs, total profit is just total revenue.

The price and quantity in a <u>monopoly</u> market would be where total profit is maximized:

P = $50

Q = 50 barrels

Π = $2500

Robin and Wills shake hands and agree to split the monopoly outcome and produce 25 barrels each for a profit of $1250 each.

There is temptation to cheat. Robin decides to produce 35 barrels. There are now 35 + 25 = 60 barrels which must sell at a lower price of $40 each. Robin's profit is now 35 ⋆ 40 = $1400, $150 more than if he had kept to the agreement. However, Wills sees his profit slip to 25 ⋆ 40 = $1000, down $250. Wills realizes that Robin has cheated on the agreement and decides to retaliate. Wills ups his production to 35 barrels. Now there are 35 + 35 = 70 barrels to sell at a price of $30 each. Robin and Wills both make 35 ⋆ 30 = $1050 profit. If Robin decided to cheat again and produce 10 more barrels, there'd be 80 barrels for sale at a market price of $20 each. Robin's profit would be 45 ⋆ $20 = $900, less than before. The same would happen if Wills contemplated cheating again.

The end result: they settle at producing 35 barrels each and making a profit of $1050. This is suboptimal but it is an equilibrium because there is no incentive for anyone to change what they're doing at this point—there is no further temptation to cheat. This is a **Nash Equilibrium**: no one can independently make themselves better off by changing their strategy (choice); you can't gain by changing what you are currently doing if no else changes, too. Everyone's strategy is their best strategy, given the strategies of everyone else.

Of course, had Robin and Wills stuck to the original agreement, they would each be making $1250 instead of $1050. The temptation to act in one's own self-interest and cheat is too great to maintain the agreement.

The inability of Robin and Wills to cooperate can be illustrated as a game (called a **prisoner's dilemma**, which we will see below). A **game** is a strategic situation where the players must consider what every other player is doing when they make their decisions about what action to take. **Game theory** is a field of study about how people behave in strategic situations.

PRISONER'S DILEMMA

Erin and Roger have been arrested for selling stolen goods on Kijiji, an offence which carries a 5-year jail term. The Crown prosecutor believes that they actually committed the theft, a crime that carries a 10-year jail term, but has no proof. In order to prosecute them for the theft, the police have to get Erin or Roger either to confess to the theft or blame the other person and be willing to testify in court against the other. They separate the pair and offer them both the same deal: If they both confess or blame the other and agree to testify, the Crown will offer them a lower sentence of 7 years. If Erin pins the blame on Roger and Roger keeps quiet, Erin will get a 2-year suspended sentence (which means *zero* jail time) for selling the stolen goods and Roger will get 10 years for the theft. The same deal holds if it's the other way around. Finally, if they both stay silent, they'll get 5 years in jail (the maximum time for selling stolen goods).

The jail terms are the **payoffs** for this game. Since jail time is bad, the players will want to minimize the time they have to serve. We assume that this is a one-time game; our players get to move once and the game is decided.

Here are their payoffs for their joint actions:

Payoffs are written as pairs. The payoffs for the player on the side are always the first number in the pair; the payoffs for the player on top are always the second number in the pair.

	Roger's Decision	
Erin's Decision	Blame	Remain Silent
Blame	(7, 7)	(0, 10)
Remain Silent	(10, 0)	(5, 5)

If Roger blames Erin, Erin's best response is to blame him (7 years versus 10 if she stays quiet). If Roger stays silent, Erin's best response is to blame him (0 time versus 5 years if she stays quiet). Erin's strategy to always blame Roger is a **dominant strategy**: a strategy chosen over all others regardless of what the other players do.

Roger has the same dominant strategy: blame Erin no matter what she does. The result is a Nash equilibrium (blame, blame) with payoffs (7, 7) years in jail.

Had they been able to keep quiet, they would only have been sentenced for 5 years each; this would have been the best result for both of them together. The Nash equilibrium is not the best (optimal) result; it is *suboptimal*.

If we set up Robin and Wills' vegetable oil production strategy as a prisoner's dilemma matrix:

	Will's Decision	
Robin's Decision	25 Barrels	35 Barrels
25 Barrels	($1250, $1250)	($1000, $1400)
35 Barrels	($1400, $1000)	($1050, $1050)

As before, Robin and Wills have the same dominant strategy: they both produce 35 barrels regardless of what the other does and each ends up with a suboptimal profit of $1050.

OLIGOPOLIES AND PUBLIC POLICY

Oligopolies are usually big companies that may be only marginally more efficient than a monopoly. The Competition Act (1985) is federal legislation meant to promote competition and prevent anti-competitive practices by Canadian businesses. For example, collusion is illegal and guilty parties can serve up to 14 years in jail or pay up to a $25-million fine or both.[2] Practices such as retail price maintenance (suppliers forcing retailers to sell at predetermined price that cannot be reduced by the retailer), tying (forcing consumers to buy another product—a tied good—if they want to buy a particular good), predatory pricing (selling goods below cost to eliminate or punish competitors), and virtually any dodgy practice by a firm aimed to restrict competition are subject to a tribunal.[3]

A Comparison of Different Market Structures			
	Perfect Competition	Monopoly	Monopolistic Competition	Oligopoly
Number of Firms	many	one	many	few
Maximize Profit	P = MR = MC	MR = MC	MR = MC	MR = MC
Price	P = MR = AR	P > MR, P = AR	P > MR, P = AR	P > MR, P = AR
Maximize Welfare	yes	no, DWL	no, DWL	no, DWL
LR Entry	yes	no	yes	very difficult
SR Positive Profits	yes	yes	yes	yes
LR Positive Profits	no	yes	no	yes
Examples	agriculture	NFL	restaurants	sugar industry

THE ALGEBRA OF OLIGOPOLY

To recap, in this chapter we have seen that firms' profits are impacted by the strategies of other firms. The best strategy for all firms is to split the monopoly outcome and maximize joint profits. But a collusive agreement like this is hard to stick to in practice because an individual firm has an incentive to cheat: If it produces more than its agreed share of the monopoly level of output, it can increase its profits. When the other firms realize there has been cheating and their profits have decreased, they will increase their output. What results is that all firms end up producing more than the monopoly outcome, receiving a lower price and earning lower profits than if they had all stuck to the collusive agreement.

EXAMPLE

There are two firms (a duopoly) facing market demand of $P = 300 - 4Q$. Both firms have a constant marginal cost and average total cost equal to $60 (MC = ATC = 60).

---

[2] Competition Act (R.S.C., 1985, c. C-34), Part VI, 45(2).
[3] Competition Act (R.S.C., 1985, c. C-34), Part VIII, 75–84.

First, suppose the market was served by a monopoly with $MR = 300 - 8Q$ and $MC = 60$.

To maximize profit, the monopoly would set $MR = MC$ and choose P and Q:

$300 - 8Q = 60$

$240 = 8Q$

$Q = 30$

$P = 300 - 4(30) = \$180$

Monopoly profit would be $(180 - 60) \star 30 = \$3600$

If our two firms colluded, they would each produce 15 units of output, and split the monopoly profit for a profit of \$1800 each.

However, there is an incentive to cheat. Suppose Firm 1 decides to cheat and produce 20 units of output. If Firm 2 continues to produce 15 units of output, there will now be $20 + 15 = 35$ units in total for sale in the market. If market $Q = 35$, the market $P = 300 - 4(35) = \$160$.

Firm 1's profit will be $(160 - 60) \star 20 = \$2000$, \$200 more than if it sticks to the agreement.

Firm 2's profit will be $(160 - 60) \star 15 = \$1500$, \$300 less than before Firm 1 cheated.

Of course Firm 2 will retaliate. It decides to also produce 20 units of output. Now there will be a total of 40 units of output for sale in the market. If market $Q = 40$, the market $P = 300 - 4(40) = \$140$.

Firm 1's profit will be $(140 - 60) \star 20 = \$1600$

Firm 2's profit will be $(140 - 60) \star 20 = \$1600$

Will either firm cheat again?

Suppose Firm 1 considers increasing its output to 25. The total market output would be 45 and market price would be $P = 300 - 4(45) = \$120$. Firm 1's profit would be $(120 - 60) \star 25 = \$1500$. Firm 1 has no incentive to produce more than 20 units of output; if it produces more it will see its profit decrease. Similarly, Firm 2 will not produce more than 20 units of output for the same reason. Both firms end up in a sub-optimal Nash equilibrium. Had they stuck to the agreement, each firm would have made \$1800 in profit but now each will only make \$1600.

KEY TERMS

oligopoly

cartel

duopoly

Nash Equilibrium

prisoner's dilemma

game

game theory

payoffs

dominant strategy

SOLVED EXAMPLE PROBLEMS

In Fruitland, strawberries are sold by 4-litre baskets to customers on a "pick-your-own" basis. There are 2 farmers who sell strawberries: Mickey and Kit. There are no costs of supplying strawberries for sale for either farmer, so each has MC = ATC = 0. Profit therefore is simply TR. Market demand for strawberries is:

P	Q	TR
12.00	25	300.00
10.75	50	537.50
10.00	75	750.00
9.00	100	900.00
8.50	125	1062.50
7.00	150	1050.00
5.50	175	962.50
4.00	200	800.00

1. If the market were served by a monopolist, what would be the quantity traded, the price per 4-litre basket, and profit for the firm?

   The monopolist will supply strawberries to maximize TR since TR = profit in the absence of any costs.

   The farmer would supply 125 baskets at a price of $8.50 per basket. Total profit is $1062.50.

2. If Mickey and Kit decide to collude, what would be their individual quantity supplied and profit?

   If they collude, they will split the monopoly outcome. They will each supply 62.5 baskets at a market price of $8.50 each; their profits will be $531.25 each.

3. Suppose Mickey and Kit agree to split the monopoly outcome. Kit, acting in her own self-interest, realizes that she can cheat and supply 87.5 baskets. What will Kit's profits be if she cheats? What will Mickey's profits be if Kit cheats?

   If Kit supplies 87.5 and Mickey sticks to the agreement and supplies 62.5 baskets, there will be a total of 87.5 + 62.5 = 150 baskets available for sale. The market price would be $7.00 per basket.

   Kit would make a profit of $7.00 ★ 87.5 = $612.50

   Mickey would make a profit of $7.00 ★ 62.5 = $437.50

   Note that if Mickey cheated and Kit did not, the profits would be the same but reversed.

4. Now suppose Mickey decides to retaliate. He increases his supply to 87.5 baskets, too. What are Mickey's and Kit's profits now?

   There are now a total of 87.5 + 87.5 = 175 baskets supplied. Market price to sell 175 baskets is $5.50.

   Mickey's profit is $5.50 ★ 87.5 = $481.25. Kit's profit will be the same.

5. Will either farmer cheat again and increase their output?

   If either Mickey or Kit decided to increase his or her supply by 25 baskets again, total quantity supplied would be 200 baskets, selling for a price of $4.00 each.

Mickey or Kit's profit (whoever cheated) would be $4.00 * 112.5 = $450.00, less than if he or she didn't cheat again.

We have a Nash equilibrium. Both farmers will supply 87.5 baskets, sell at a price of $5.50, and earn a profit of $481.25. Had they not cheated and stuck to the original agreement to split the monopoly outcome, they would have each earned $531.25 profit.

The Nash equilibrium is sub-optimal.

6. Illustrate the Nash equilibrium as a prisoner's dilemma matrix.

Mickey's Decision

		62.5 Baskets	87.5 Baskets
Kit's Decision	62.5 Baskets	($531.25, $531.25)	($437.50, $612.50)
	87.5 Baskets	($612.50, $437.50)	(($481.25, $481.25))

PROBLEMS

1. Two big sugar processing companies, Northern Foods and Pacific Sugars, are planning on expanding their operations to Canada. Both are deciding whether to build one plant or two.

   If they both build one plant, each firm will make $8 million in profit. If they both build two plants, each firm will make $6 million in profit. If one firm builds one firm and the other builds two plants, the firm that builds one plant will make $5 million in profit while the one the builds two plants will earn $9 million in profit.

   a) Model this decision-making problem as a prisoner's dilemma matrix.

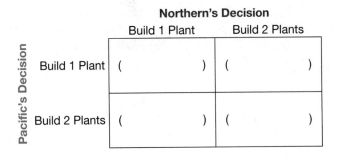

   b) What would be the optimal strategy for each firm?

   c) What are the Nash equilibrium solution and payoffs?

   d) Does any firm have a dominant strategy?

2. Steve and Michelle are farmers who sell their surplus manure to other local farmers. Manure is sold by the cubic yard (dirt, soil, mulch etc are often sold by this measurement). Steve and Michelle have no costs of production (buyers come and pick up their manure themselves). Market demand is given as $P = 20 - Q$, $MR = 20 - 2Q$, and $MC = ATC = 0$.

   a) If Steve and Michelle agree to split the monopoly outcome, how much would each farmer produce and what would be their individual profits?

   b) Suppose Steve decides to cheat on the agreement and produces 7 cubic yards. What is Steve's profit now? What is Michelle's profit now?

   c) Suppose Michelle considers retaliation and thinks about producing 7 cubic yards? What would her and Steve's profits be in this case? Should Michelle retaliate?

   d) Illustrate the Nash equilibrium as a prisoner's dilemma matrix.

Steve's Decision

	Produce 5	Produce 7
Produce 5	( )	( )
Produce 7	( )	( )

Michelle's Decision

SOLUTIONS

1. Two big sugar processing companies, Northern Foods and Pacific Sugars, are planning on expanding their operations to Canada. Both are deciding whether to build one plant or two.

    If they both build one plant, each firm will make $8 million in profit. If they both build two plants, each firm will make $6 million in profit. If one firm builds one firm and the other builds two plants, the firm that builds one plant will make $5 million in profit while the one the builds two plants will earn $9 million in profit.

    a) Model this decision-making problem as a prisoner's dilemma matrix.

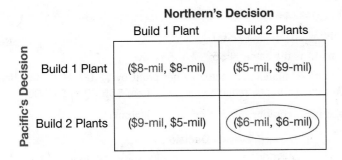

Northern's Decision

	Build 1 Plant	Build 2 Plants
Build 1 Plant	($8-mil, $8-mil)	($5-mil, $9-mil)
Build 2 Plants	($9-mil, $5-mil)	($6-mil, $6-mil)

(Pacific's Decision)

   b) What would be the optimal strategy for each firm?

   They should split the monopoly outcome and each build 1 plant. They would earn a profit of $8 million each.

   c) What are the Nash equilibrium solution and payoffs?

   The Nash equilibrium is for each to build 2 plants and each earn a profit of $6 million. This is a sub-optimal solution.

   d) Does any firm have a dominant strategy?

   Both firms have the same dominant strategy: Build 2 plants. It doesn't matter what the other firm does, each firm, acting in its own self-interest, will choose to build 2 plants to maximize its individual profit.

2. Steve and Michelle are farmers who sell their surplus manure to other local farmers. Manure is sold by the cubic yard (dirt, soil, mulch etc are often sold by this measurement). Steve and Michelle have no costs of production (buyers come and pick up their manure themselves). Market demand is given as $P = 20 - Q$, $MR = 20 - 2Q$, and $MC = ATC = 0$.

   a) If Steve and Michelle agree to split the monopoly outcome, how much would each farmer produce and what would be their individual profits?

   The monopoly would produce where its $MR = MC$:

   $20 - 2Q = 0$

   $20 = 2Q$

   $Q = 10$ cubic yards

   $P = 20 - Q = 20 - 10 = 10

   They would each produce 5 cubic yards, sell it at $P = 10, and make a profit of $50 each.

b) Suppose Steve decides to cheat on the agreement and produces 7 cubic yards. What is Steve's profit now? What is Michelle's profit now?

If Steve produces 7, there will be a total of 7 + 5 = 12 cubic yards for sale.

Market P = 20 – 12 = $8

Steve's profit = $8 * 7 = $56.00

Michelle's profit = $8 * 5 = $40.00

(If Michelle had cheated instead, the profits would be the same but reversed.)

c) Suppose Michelle considers retaliation and thinks about producing 7 cubic yards? What would her and Steve's profits be in this case? Should Michelle retaliate?

Total market Q = 7 + 7 = 14 cubic yards

Market P = 20 – 14 = $6

Steve's profit = $6 * 7 = $42.00

Michelle's profit is the same = $6 * 7 = $42.00

Michelle should retaliate. She increases her profit by $2.00. Her retaliation punishes Steve for cheating by reducing his profit from $56.00 to $42.00.

d) Illustrate the Nash equilibrium as a prisoner's dilemma matrix.

Steve's Decision

		Produce 5	Produce 7
Michelle's Decision	Produce 5	($50.00, $50.00)	($40.00, $56.00)
	Produce 7	($56.00, $40.00)	(($42.00, $42.00))

CHAPTER 12

Markets for Resources

MAIN CONCEPTS AND DEFINITIONS

Producers have to get the resources they need to produce their output from somewhere. They go to the **markets for factors of production**: the labour market, the capital market, and the land market. Since we've used labour as our main input into the production process, let's start with a look at the labour market.

LABOUR MARKET

We assume that the labour market is competitive: firms and workers are **price takers**. The wage is the equilibrium wage determined by market forces. For example, think about the fast-food industry. Employees expect to be paid the going (usually the minimum) wage and employers expect to pay that.

LABOUR DEMAND

A firm will hire workers as long as the last worker hired doesn't cost the firm more than the output they produce adds to the firm's revenue. A worker's addition to revenue is the amount of money that the goods he or she added to total output (that he or she produced) bring in when sold. The amount of goods a worker adds is his or her marginal product, MP_L. The addition to total revenue of each good sold is their marginal revenue MR. The worker's total contribution to the firm's revenue is therefore $MR \star MP_L$. We now define **marginal revenue product: $MRP = MR \star MP_L$**, the contribution to a firm's total revenue made by the last worker hired. In a competitive goods market, MR = P so $MRP = P \star MP_L$. Recall that as more workers are hired, MP diminishes and therefore MRP diminishes.

   The addition to the cost of a worker is the wage, w, the firm pays. You can think of the wage as the MC of a worker. You can think of the MRP, the contribution to total revenue of the worker's output, as the worker's MR. As long as the addition to total revenue outweighs the addition to total cost, that worker will be hired. The firm will hire workers up to the point where w = MRP: where the MC of the worker (w) equals the MR (the worker's contribution to total revenue, MRP).

EXAMPLE: JERRY'S NACHOS

Jerry sells nachos from a kiosk at the Air Canada Centre during hockey and basketball games and concerts. Nachos sell at a price of $4 each serving; there are many nacho kiosks so the market is competitive. The going wage is $13 per hour and each shift is 6 hours, so each employee will be paid $13 * 6 = $78 per shift (their wage is $78 per shift).

Jerry's nacho and labour data per 6-hour shift are as follows:

L	Q	MP	MRP	W
0	0			
1	60	60	240	78
2	90	50	200	78
3	135	45	180	78
4	170	35	140	78
5	190	20	80	78
6	204	14	56	78
7	185	−19	−76	78

Jerry will hire 5 workers. The MRP > w for the 5th worker hired. Jerry would never hire the 6th worker; the 6th worker's contribution to revenue is only $56 but would cost Jerry $78 (he'd be losing money).

At any wage level, Jerry will simply equate the wage to MRP to find the quantity of labour he wants to hire. The MRP is the demand curve for labour.

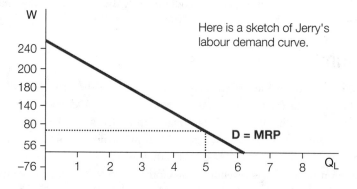

Here is a sketch of Jerry's labour demand curve.

A change in the wage rate, w, is a movement along the demand for labour curve, a change in the quantity demanded of labour. Anything that changes the MR (or the P) of the good or the MP of the workers is a change in the demand for labour that will shift the demand curve.

LABOUR SUPPLY

When someone chooses to work an hour, they give up an hour of leisure. Leisure is any time spent not working for pay—watching a movie, going for dinner, doing your laundry, sleeping—to name just a few leisure activities. In order to get an hour of leisure, you have to give up one hour of work and therefore give up one hour's wage. The opportunity cost of an hour of leisure is an hour's wage. The higher the hourly wage, the more expensive is an hour of leisure. Leisure is a normal good, so the higher the wage (the price of leisure) and income, the less leisure and more work hours will be supplied. In other words, the higher the wage, the greater the quantity of labour supplied and the labour supply curve is upward sloping.

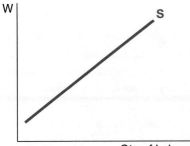

Qty of Labour

A change in the wage rate, w, is a movement along the supply curve, a change in the quantity supplied of labour. There will be a change in supply—a shift of the supply curve—if something other than the wage changes that affects labour supply. For instance, if there is immigration (an influx of new workers), a change in society's attitudes where new groups of workers enter the labour force (like women after WWII), or a new opportunity arises and workers are mobile and go to a new market, the labour supply curve will shift accordingly.

When D for labour = S of labour, the labour market is in equilibrium:

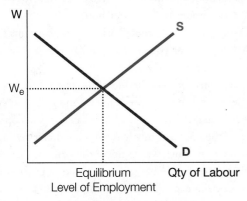

Equilibrium   Qty of Labour
Level of Employment

MINIMUM WAGES

When the government believes equilibrium wage is too low, it can set a minimum wage—a wage floor—to ensure at least a certain wage level for lower income earners. A minimum wage results in unemployment; the greater the minimum, the more unemployment.

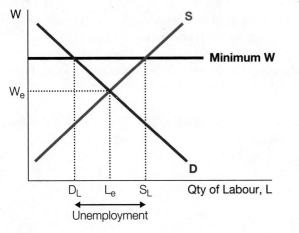

OTHER RESOURCE MARKETS

The purchase of capital equipment and land generally are longer-term investments. The firm must consider not only their contribution to revenue today but also throughout the life of the resources. In other words, consider not only the current marginal revenue product of the resource but also the <u>expected</u> marginal revenue product in each period the resource is used.

Let's focus on capital equipment. Just like labour, capital has a marginal product. Consider a copier in a print shop. You press a button and the copier does the rest, printing out, say, flyers for a customer. If it prints out 500 flyers in an hour that sell for $0.11 each, the copier's hourly MRP = $0.11 $\star$ 500 = $55.

What does the copier get paid? Consider that the copier eventually will wear down and have to be replaced. The firm owns the copier for only a certain time, as if it rents the copier and replaces it (rents a new one) once the original breaks down beyond repair. We say that capital, denoted K, commands a **rental price, r:** an amount paid to use a resource for a limited time. So, what is r? It's the market value of the resource. If you spent $2000 on the copier which will last 1 year and is used for 100 hours per week, the hourly cost of the copier is $2000 divided by 52 weeks $\star$ 100 hours = $0.39 per hour.

A firm will hire capital up to the point where the rental price of capital equals its marginal revenue product—where r = MRP_K. In our copier example, $0.39 < $55 so the firm will purchase more copiers, other things being equal.

The MRP of capital likely won't remain constant over the life of the piece. Our copier will need more and more servicing as it ages, and the increased down time means its MP will fall over time. The fall in MP will reduce its MRP, so as it ages, we expect the copier's MRP to decline. We wouldn't want to "pay" the copier as much as we did when it was new.

How much will we pay to buy capital equipment? We compare the price we have to pay for it to its expected contribution to our total revenue, taking into consideration the interest rate. If you borrow the money to buy the capital, you have to pay it back plus the interest. If you pay cash, the interest rate is what you could have earned on that money had you instead invested it, so it counts toward the opportunity cost of the capital purchase. Either way, the interest rate affects the real price of capital.

PRESENT VALUE

Present value, PV, is the amount of money needed today to produce a given amount of money at a specified future date, accounting for the prevailing interest rate.

For example, I want to invest some money today so that in 5 years, I'll end up with $4000. The interest rate is 7% and expected to remain at 7% for the next 5 years. How much do I have to invest today?

$$PV = \frac{X}{(1 + i)^t}$$ where X = amount you want to receive in period t at the going interest rate, i.

$$PV = \frac{400}{(1 + .07)^5}$$

$$= 2851.94$$

This means that to get $4000 in 5 years, I invest $2851.19 today at a 7% interest rate.

If I also want to receive $100 for each of the five years and get my $4000 in the fifth year, the formula changes. The $100 (whatever dollar amount) annual payment is called a **coupon** payment, denoted C. The new present value formula is

$$PV = \frac{C}{(1 + i)} + \frac{C}{(1 + i)^2} + \ldots + \frac{C}{(1 + i)^t} + \frac{X}{(1 + i)^t}$$

$$PV = \frac{100}{(1 + .07)} + \frac{100}{(1 + .07)^2} + \frac{100}{(1 + .07)^3} + \frac{100}{(1 + .07)^4} + \frac{100}{(1 + .07)^5} + \frac{4000}{(1 + .07)^5}$$

= $3261.96 Invest $3261.96 today to get a total of $4500 in 5 years.

Suppose a firm is choosing between two new technologies for its factory. It can pay cash so we don't have to worry about paying interest on a loan. Technology A has a lifespan of 10 years and an expected MRP of $12 000 for each and every year of its life. It costs the firm $75 000 to purchase. Technology B has a lifespan of 8 years but an expected MRP of $14 000 for each and every year of its life. It also costs $75 000 to purchase. The interest rate is 8% and expected to prevail for the next 10 years. Which technology should the firm buy?

The firm will choose the technology that has the highest present value; that's the one that's worth the most to the firm today. Each year, the technology will contribute its MRP to the firm, just like getting a coupon payment if you're an investor (the firm *is* an investor—it's investing in a new technology). If the firm spends $75 000 on the technology, it wants to get as much out of the technology as it can (at least get the $75 000 it spends back, hopefully more). If the firm spends $75 000 today, what does it get out of the technology in total over its lifetime?

We compute the present value of each technology, and the firm will chose the one that delivers the most for the $75 000 spent today.

For Technology A:

$$PV = \frac{12\ 000}{(1 + .08)} + \frac{12\ 000}{(1 + .08)^2} + \ldots + \frac{12\ 000}{(1 + .08)^{10}}$$

= $80 520.98

For Technology B:

$$PV = \frac{14\ 000}{(1 + .08)} + \frac{14\ 000}{(1 + .08)^2} + \ldots + \frac{14\ 000}{(1 + .08)^8}$$

= $80 452.95

Technology A has a higher present value than Technology B. The firm should buy A; it will spend $75 000 but get back $80 520.98 in contributions to total revenue from that technology.

If the PV is less than purchase price, don't make the investment; you'll never recover the money you spent.

Note that the decision to purchase land is analogous to the capital purchasing decision.

markets for factors of production
price takers
marginal revenue product: MRP =
    MR $\star$ MP$_L$

rental price, r
present value, PV
coupon

SOLVED EXAMPLE PROBLEMS

1. Sly's Subs is a sub sandwich shop in Strathmore, AB. It sells its 6" subs in a competitive market for $5.25 each. Sly pays his employees the equilibrium wage rate of $11.00 per hour for an 8-hour shift. The table below shows Sly's production function for subs for an 8-hour shift and leaves room for you to fill in some missing numbers:

L	Q	MP	MRP	WAGE
0	0		0	
1	50			
2		35		
3		20		
4		14		
5	128			
6	122			

a) Fill in the table.

The wage is $11.00 per hour for an 8-hour shift = $88 per shift per worker.

The market is competitive, so P = MR. So, the MRP = P * MP = 5.25 * MP.

L	Q	MP	MRP	WAGE
0	0		0	88
1	50	50	262.5	88
2	85	35	183.75	88
3	105	20	105	88
4	119	14	73.5	88
5	128	9	47.25	88
6	122	–6	–31.5	88

b) How many workers will Sly hire?

Sly will hire up to the point where w = MRP. Since w doesn't equal MRP anywhere, Sly will hire the last worker where MRP > w. This way, the worker's contribution to revenue exceeds her contribution to total cost and therefore she adds to Sly's profit. Sly will hire 3 workers.

c) Suppose the province imposed a minimum wage rate of $13.50 per hour. How many workers would Sly hire now?

L	Q	MP	MRP	WAGE
0	0		0	108
1	50	50	262.5	108
2	85	35	183.75	108
3	105	20	105	108
4	119	14	73.5	108
5	128	9	47.25	108
6	122	−6	−31.5	108

The wage increase means that Sly now pays each worker $108.00 for an 8-hour shift. Sly would only hire 2 workers. He wouldn't hire the third employee; he'd add $108 to total cost but only add $105 to total revenue. Sly would lose money if he hired worker #3.

d) Assume that the supply curve is a typically upward-sloping curve (whether it's linear doesn't matter). Sketch the labour market for Sly's Subs based on the *hourly* wage rates before and after the minimum wage was imposed. For simplicity, just sketch the labour demand curve as a linear function.

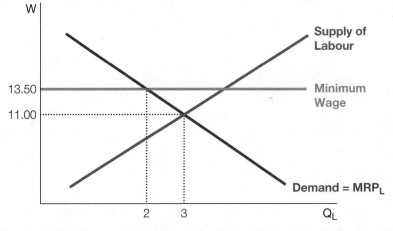

2. A firm is deciding between two new technologies for its plant. Each costs $83 000. Technology A has an expected MRP of $14 000 for each year of its 9-year lifetime. Technology B has an expected MRP of $16 600 for each year of its 7-year lifetime. The annual interest rate is assumed to be constant over the next 10 years at 3%. Which technology should the firm purchase?

For Technology A:

$$PV = \frac{14\ 000}{(1 + .03)} + \frac{14\ 000}{(1 + .03)^2} + \frac{14\ 000}{(1 + .03)^3} + \frac{14\ 000}{(1 + .03)^4} + \ldots + \frac{14\ 000}{(1 + .03)^9} = \$109\ 005.52$$

For Technology B:

$$PV = \frac{16\ 600}{(1 + .03)} + \frac{16\ 600}{(1 + .03)^2} + \frac{16\ 600}{(1 + .03)^3} + \frac{16\ 600}{(1 + .03)^4} + \ldots + \frac{16\ 600}{(1 + .03)^7} = \$103\ 422.70$$

The firm should buy Technology A because it has the highest present value. For the $83 000 the firm spends on a new technology, Technology A will return $5582.82 more in additions to total revenue than will Technology B, discounting for the interest rate. In total, Technology A returns $26 005.52 above its $83 000 cost.

1. Master Manufacturing produces coloured pencils which sell competitively at $0.80 each. The current equilibrium wage rate is $12.00 per hour. Here is the firm's production function:

L	Q	MP	MRP	WAGE
0	0		0	
1		20		
2		30		
3	75			
4		18		
5	108			
6	119			

a) Fill in the table.

b) How many workers will Master Manufacturing hire?

c) Suppose the firm's workers unionize and negotiate a new wage rate of $15.00 per hour. How many workers will the firm hire now?

2. A firm is deciding between two new technologies for its plant. Each costs $72 000. Technology A has an expected MRP of $21 000 for each year of its 6-year lifetime. Technology B has an expected MRP of $23 250 for each year of its 5-year lifetime. The annual interest rate is assumed to be constant over the next 8 years at 4%. Which technology should the firm purchase?

1. Master Manufacturing produces coloured pencils which sell competitively at $0.80 each. The current equilibrium wage rate is $12.00 per hour. Here is the firm's production function:

L	Q	MP	MRP	WAGE
0	0		0	12
1	20	20	16	12
2	50	30	24	12
3	75	25	20	12
4	93	18	14.4	12
5	108	15	12	12
6	119	11	8.8	12

a) Fill in the table.

b) How many workers will Master Manufacturing hire?

   The firm will hire workers such that w = MRP. This happens with the 5th worker hired.

c) Suppose the firm's workers unionize and negotiate a new wage rate of $15.00 per hour. How many workers will the firm hire now?

   Here's the table with the new wage rate:

L	Q	MP	MRP	WAGE
0	0		0	15
1	20	20	16	15
2	50	30	24	15
3	75	25	20	15
4	93	18	14.4	15
5	108	15	12	15
6	119	11	8.8	15

   Now the firm will only hire 3 workers (where MRP > w). It wouldn't hire the 4th worker because the 4th worker would add more to total cost ($15) than to total revenue ($14.40).

2. A firm is deciding between two new technologies for its plant. Each costs $72 000. Technology A has an expected MRP of $21 000 for each year of its 6-year lifetime. Technology B has an expected MRP of $23 250 for each year of its 5-year lifetime. The annual interest rate is assumed to be constant over the next 8 years at 4%. Which technology should the firm purchase?

   For Technology A:

   $$PV = \frac{21\ 000}{(1+.04)} + \frac{21\ 000}{(1+.04)^2} + \frac{21\ 000}{(1+.04)^3} + \frac{21\ 000}{(1+.04)^4} + \ldots + \frac{21\ 000}{(1+.04)^6} = \$110\ 084.87$$

   For Technology B:

   $$PV = \frac{23\ 250}{(1+.04)} + \frac{23\ 250}{(1+.04)^2} + \frac{23\ 250}{(1+.04)^3} + \frac{23\ 250}{(1+.04)^4} + \frac{23\ 250}{(1+.04)^5} = \$103\ 504.87$$

   The firm should purchase Technology A. It adds $38 084.87 to total revenue above its cost; Technology B only adds $31 504.87.

CHAPTER 13
Consumer Theory

MAIN CONCEPTS AND DEFINITIONS

When we purchase and consume goods and services, we derive satisfaction from them (whether it's enjoyment or simply usefulness). We call this satisfaction **utility** and measure it in units called utils. The set of all the goods and services someone consumes is their **consumption bundle**. Just as firms try to maximize their profits, consumers try to maximize their utility.

Every individual values consumption bundles differently than others. For example, you may get a total of 2000 utils from attending eight Green Bay Packers home games while the person sitting next to you only gets 740 utils. Where do these numbers come from? They come from the utility function that every individual has. Think of it as an equation in our head: We plug in how many of each good we consume and the equation calculates the total utility we get from that consumption bundle. (In second-year microeconomics we work with "real" utility functions.)

EXAMPLE: PIZZA CONSUMPTION

Aaron loves pizza. He's hungry. The first slice he eats gives him great satisfaction. The second slice makes him even happier because he's starting to get full. With each subsequent slice he eats, his total satisfaction has increased, but after the second slice, each slice doesn't taste quite as good as the last one because he's really starting to get full. He gets to the point where the last slice he eats is too much and now he doesn't feel so good. That last slice actually took away from his total satisfaction with the meal.

Aaron measures his utility from pizza and derives his total utility for pizza as he consumes more and more slices:

Q	TU
0	0
1	28
2	60
3	78
4	90
5	100
6	90

Aaron's TU increases up to the 5th slice.

By then he's so full that eating the 6th slice makes him worse off than if he had stopped at 5 slices.

Each additional slice (up to slice #5) adds to his total utility. We define **marginal utility, MU**, as the increase in total utility from consuming one more good. MU is the slope of the TU function. TU is maximized when MU = 0.

Q	TU	MU
0	0	
1	28	28
2	60	32
3	78	18
4	90	12
5	100	10
6	90	−10

Notice that after the second slice, we have **diminishing MU**:

Each additional unit of a good consumed adds less to TU than the previous one.

Here's Aaron's total utility for pizza function. Does this remind you of the total product function we saw earlier in the course?

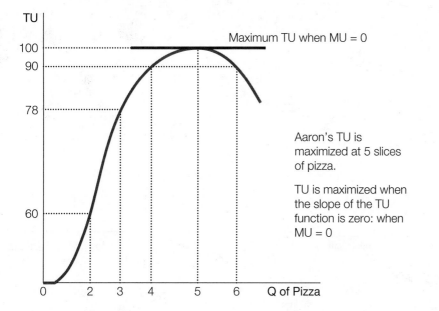

Maximum TU when MU = 0

Aaron's TU is maximized at 5 slices of pizza.

TU is maximized when the slope of the TU function is zero: when MU = 0

This is a representative TU function for the consumption of only one good. Let's now consider more than one good (clearly more realistic) and let's also think about limitations to what we can consume.

BUDGET CONSTRAINT

We like stuff. The more we can consume of stuff we like, the happier (more utility) we get from our consumption bundle. However, we can't consume as much as we'd *like* to consume because we face two constraints on our spending:

- **Income constraint**: We can only consume what we can afford (no credit allowed).
- **Price constraint**: How much we can consume of a good, given our income, depends on the price of the good.

Since consuming more of the goods we like makes us more satisfied, we want to buy as much as we can. This means we'll be spending all of the income we've allotted to purchasing our consumption bundle. Given our income and the prices of goods, we can depict all the possible combinations of goods we can buy if we spend all of our income. This is our **budget constraint, BC**.

Suppose that Aaron has an income of $1500 which he can spend on tickets to hockey games and basketball games.

P_h = price of hockey tickets = $125 per ticket

P_b = price of basketball tickets = $75 per ticket

If Q_h = quantity of hockey tickets and Q_b = quantity of basketball tickets, Aaron's BC is:

$125Q_h + 75Q_b = 1500$ (what he spends on hockey and basketball tickets = his income)

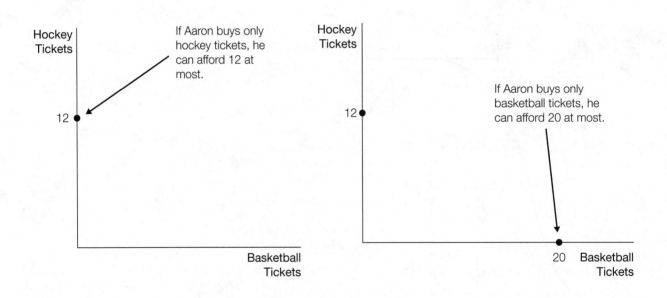

If we join up the two intercepts, we get Aaron's budget constraint:

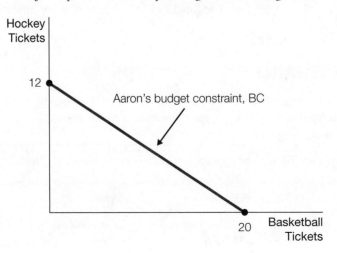

The general equation for a BC for 2 goods X and Y and income N is:

Px * X + Py * Y = N

The slope of the BC is $\dfrac{-Px}{Py}$

The x-intercept is N/Px

The y-intercept is N/Py

Px/Py is the **relative price** of the goods: to get 1 good X, how many of good Y must be given up. This is the **opportunity cost** of good X in terms of good Y. The |slope| of the budget constraint is the opportunity cost of good X (the good on the horizontal axis). Does this remind you of a PPF?

CHANGES TO THE BUDGET CONSTRAINT

Any change to the consumer's income or the price of either or both goods will change the budget constraint.

If income N increases: BC shifts right (parallel shift). You can buy more of either or both goods.

If income N decreases: BC shifts left (parallel shift). You can't buy as much as before.

If Px increases, BC rotates in (no change in the Y-intercept). You can't buy as much of good X as before.

If Px decreases: BC rotates out (no change in the Y-intercept). You can buy more of good X now.

If Py increases: BC rotates in (no change to the X-intercept). You can't buy as much of good Y as before.

If Py decreases: BC rotates out (no change in the X-intercept). You can buy more of good Y now.

If Px and Py both change in the same direction by the same proportion: You can buy more (or less) of either or both goods, just like you had an increase (or decrease) in income. BC shifts right (or left), a parallel shift.

If Px and Py both change by different magnitudes regardless of direction, BC will rotate appropriately.

Some examples of changes in the budget constraint:

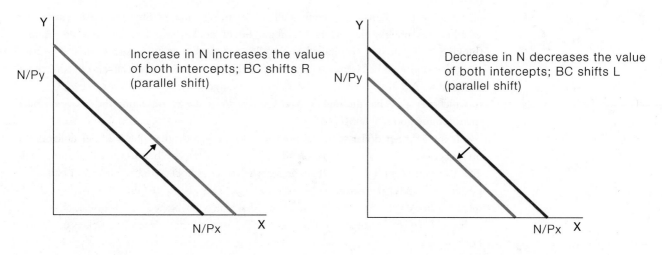

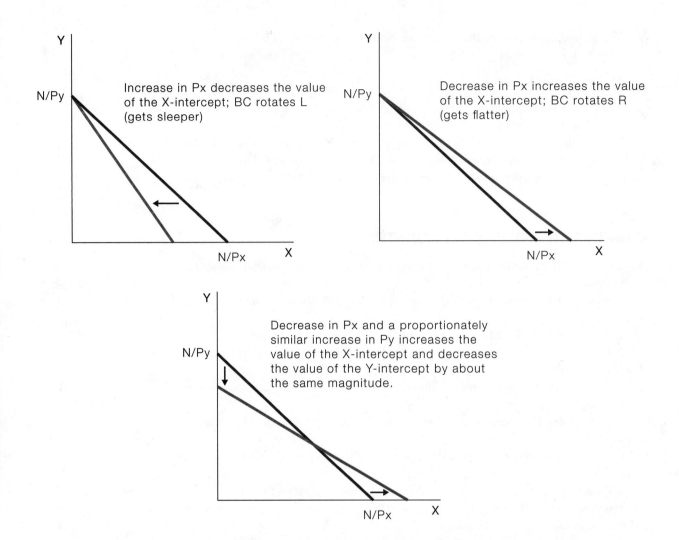

All combinations of goods on or inside the budget constraint are affordable. These combinations constitute the consumer's **budget set**. But which combination will maximize total utility?

Assume that Aaron is spending all of his ticket budget. Suppose he is examining whether he's bought the "right" combination of hockey and basketball tickets. Aaron, thinking at the margin, considers how he allocated the last dollar he spent: Should he have spent that dollar on hockey tickets or on basketball tickets? Since he wants to maximize his TU he'll want to have spent that dollar on whatever good will add the most to his TU—that is, whichever good has the highest MU for that dollar spent. We define the MU per dollar spent for any good X as **MUx/Px**.

If the MU per dollar spent on hockey tickets is greater than the MU per dollar spent on basketball tickets, Aaron will spend that dollar on hockey because it adds more to his TU than if he spent it on basketball; he'll consume more hockey tickets and fewer basketball tickets. If the MU per dollar spent on basketball tickets is greater than the MU per dollar spent on hockey tickets, Aaron will spend that dollar on basketball because it adds more to his TU than if he spent it on hockey; he'll consume more basketball tickets and fewer hockey tickets.

When the MU per dollar spent is the same for both goods, buying more of one good over the other makes no difference to TU. What you'd add to TU from buying a dollar's worth of one good is exactly offset by the reduction in TU from giving up a dollar's worth of the other good. Changing the consumption bundle will not add any more to TU, so TU must be at a maximum. Therefore, TU is maximized when **MUx/Px = MUy/Py**. We'd equate the MU/P for every good, no matter how many there are in the consumption bundle.

CONSUMER PREFERENCES

We haven't yet considered an individual's preferences when it comes to choosing their consumption bundle. For example, Aaron can have various affordable combinations of hockey games and basketball games per week that would make him equally satisfied and give him the same TU. For instance, 1 basketball and 3 hockey games, or 3 hockey games and 2 basketball games are combos that may give him a TU of say, 47. Aaron would be indifferent as to which combo he had if he were just looking to get TU = 47.

We can graph all the combinations of hockey tickets and basketball tickets that give Aaron the same TU on something we call an **indifference curve, IC**. Here's a typical IC map (more than one IC in a diagram):

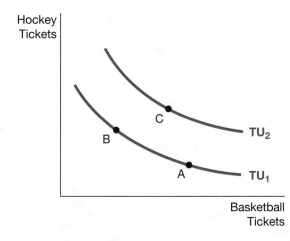

FOUR PROPERTIES OF INDIFFERENCE CURVES

1. Higher ICs yield a higher TU. Check out the above diagram. At point C, Aaron can consume more of both kinds of tickets compared to point B on TU1. At any point on TU_2, more tickets in total are consumed. More is better and therefore more is preferred. Having more stuff gives you more utility, so TU is higher the more you consume (assuming, of course, that you like the goods you're consuming).

2. ICs slope downward. Suppose you were consuming the quantity of hockey tickets at point B. If someone wanted you to give up some of those hockey tickets, they'd have to give you more basketball tickets to make up for the hockey tickets you give up if you're going to maintain the <u>same</u> level of TU. If you just gave up some hockey tickets without getting more basketball tickets, you'd have fewer tickets in total and a lower TU.

3. ICs don't cross each other. If they did, there'd be an intersection point where there'd be a consumption bundle on two ICs with two different TU values. You can't have that. Every consumption bundle has a unique TU ranking.

4. Most indifference curves are convex to the origin. They're not linear. That's because for most goods, the less you have of a good, the harder it is to give up some of it and you'd want more of another good to compensate. For example, it's not a big deal to give up a chocolate brownie if you have 4 dozen; you'd likely be willing to trade a brownie for a couple of cookies. If you only have 3 brownies, it's harder to part with one and you'd want a lot more than a couple of cookies to get you to give up another brownie and still retain the same level of TU. The goods are substitutable, but the terms of trade change along the IC.

There are 2 exceptions to the convex generalization we made above. Goods that are **perfect substitutes** always trade off for each other at the same rate. For example, you'll always trade 4 quarters to get a loonie, no matter how many quarters or loonies you have. The rate of trade is constant. The IC would be linear for perfect substitutes. Goods that are **perfect complements** don't have a rate of trade. Think of a hot dog bun and a frankfurter. One bun plus one frankfurter make a hot dog that gives you some level of TU. If you only have one bun, having all the frankfurters in the world won't give you more hot dog utility because you'll still only have one hot dog. Same for having one frankfurter; 5000 buns won't give you any more hotdogs if you only have one frankfurter. To get more TU, you have to get more complete hot dogs. The IC would look like a letter L where the only combinations that matter are the ones on the corners.

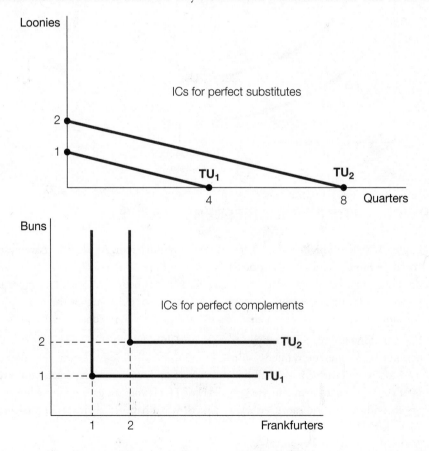

MAXIMIZING TOTAL UTILITY

We still haven't decided how to choose the optimal consumption bundle. What we know is that individuals have preferences about what they like and what kind of satisfaction they get from different combinations of the things they like and consume. To maximize TU means consuming a bundle of goods that's on the highest possible IC.

We also know that individuals are constrained in how much they buy (consume) by their income and the prices of the goods they purchase. More stuff is better, so they will want to spend all of their income to buy the most goods they can. To maximize TU also means consuming a bundle of goods that's on the budget constraint.

Now we've got it: the optimal consumption bundle is on the BC and on the highest possible IC. This happens when we're on the IC that is just tangent to the BC.

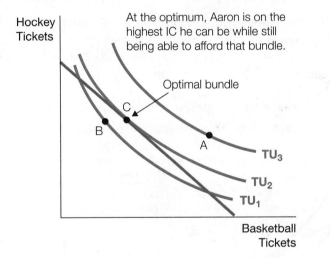

At the optimum, Aaron is on the highest IC he can be while still being able to afford that bundle.

Any bundle like A, for example, on TU_3 is not affordable (above the BC).

Any point like B is inside the BC; Aaron can spend more money, buy more tickets and get a higher TU.

Point C is the point of tangency of TU_2 to the BC, Aaron's optimal consumption bundle.

At point C, the BC and IC are just tangent. That means the slope of the BC equals the slope of the IC at point C. They're both negative, so we can drop the minus signs. But also recall, we **maximize TU by setting MUx/Px = MUy/Py**. If we rearrange this equality, we get MUx/MUy = Px/Py. Px/Py is the |slope of the BC|. That means MUx/MUy must be the |slope of the IC| and equal to P_X/P_Y at the point of tangency. We can now find the optimal consumption bundle by setting the slope of the IC = slope of the BC; that is, by setting MUx/MUy = Px/Py.

The slope of the IC is called the **marginal rate of substitution, MRS**. It tells us how much of good Y you have to get t   o compensate for giving up one good X and keep the same level of TU. So, MRS = MUx/MUy.

CHANGES TO THE BC

Since the optimal consumption bundle happens at the tangency of the BC and IC, anything that changes the BC will change the point of tangency and there'll be a new optimal bundle of goods. We can see how this works using diagrams.

Example: An increase in income, N

We'll let basketball tickets be the X good and hockey tickets be the Y good.

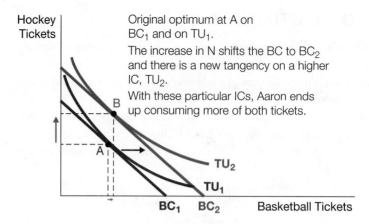

Original optimum at A on BC$_1$ and on TU$_1$.

The increase in N shifts the BC to BC$_2$ and there is a new tangency on a higher IC, TU$_2$.

With these particular ICs, Aaron ends up consuming more of both tickets.

NOTE: Where the new tangency happens depends on what the ICs look like. Everyone has unique preferences so their IC maps will all look different. It's possible that the increase in N could lead to more of one good and less of the other being consumed at the new tangency point. It all depends on how we draw the ICs.

Example: A decrease in the price of basketball tickets, P$_X$

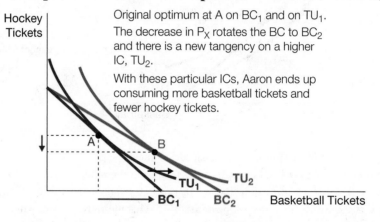

Original optimum at A on BC$_1$ and on TU$_1$.

The decrease in P$_X$ rotates the BC to BC$_2$ and there is a new tangency on a higher IC, TU$_2$.

With these particular ICs, Aaron ends up consuming more basketball tickets and fewer hockey tickets.

Example: An increase in the price of hockey tickets, P$_Y$

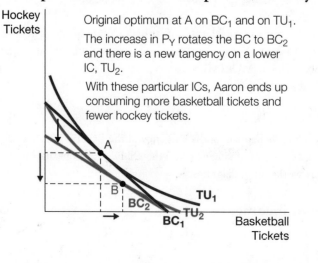

Original optimum at A on BC$_1$ and on TU$_1$.

The increase in P$_Y$ rotates the BC to BC$_2$ and there is a new tangency on a lower IC, TU$_2$.

With these particular ICs, Aaron ends up consuming more basketball tickets and fewer hockey tickets.

SUBSTITUTION AND INCOME EFFECTS

Whenever the price of a good changes, there are two effects on the consumption of that good.

Substitution Effect: We want to buy more of the now relatively cheaper good and less of the now relatively more expensive good. This is a movement to another position on the same TU curve. We choose a new bundle that would be tangent to the BC that results from the price change.

Income Effect: The change in the price of the good changes our purchasing power. It's as if our income has changed. The change in purchasing power is what puts the optimal bundle on another BC, much like a change in income does.

Originally we are at an optimal consumption bundle at point A.

The price of basketball tickets decreases and there is a new tangency to another indifference curve and a new optimal bundle at C.

Draw an imaginary budget line that is parallel to the new budget line and just tangent to the original indifference curve—the original curve is the blue one and the imaginary budget line is in black.

The imaginary budget line shows what the new consumption bundle would be at the *new* relative prices *keeping the same original level of utility*.

It shows how we would substitute relatively cheaper basketball tickets for hockey tickets to maintain the same utility level. This is the movement from A to B.

We get from B to C because the decrease in the price of basketball tickets increased our purchasing power. It's like we have more money to spend in general because we don't have to spend as much on basketball tickets as before.

This "increase in our budget" lets us consume on a higher indifference curve.

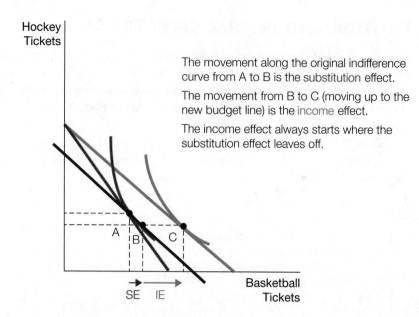

The movement along the original indifference curve from A to B is the substitution effect.

The movement from B to C (moving up to the new budget line) is the income effect.

The income effect always starts where the substitution effect leaves off.

DERIVING THE DEMAND CURVE

We just saw how the optimal quantity of basketball tickets changed when the price of basketball tickets changed. If we repeat this exercise by changing ticket prices to a variety of prices and noting the optimal quantity for each price, we get the link between price and quantity demanded.

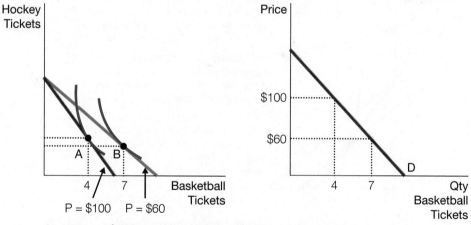

At a price of $100 per ticket, Aaron chooses 4 basketball tickets.
At a lower price of $60 per ticket, Aaron chooses 7 basketball tickets.

THE ALGEBRA OF CONSUMER CHOICE

We have seen that a consumer choosing a bundle of two goods, good X and good Y, will maximize TU by choosing quantities of X and Y such that the marginal utility per dollar spent on X (MUx/Px) equals the marginal utility per dollar spent on Y (MUy/Py). Diagrammatically this is the same as choosing quantities of X and Y such that the |slope of the budget constraint|, Px/Py equals the |slope of the highest possible indifference curve|, MUx/MUy. That is, the point of tangency where the slopes of the two curves are equal occurs when MUx/MUy = Px/Py. If we rearrange this tangency condition we get MUx/Px = MUy/Py. In other words, the tangency condition is the same as equating the marginal utility per dollar spent on each good.

For those of you who are interested, here's a more formal explanation why the slope of the IC = MUx/MUy:

For 2 goods X and Y (on the usual x and y axes respectively), the slope of the indifference curve is $\Delta y/\Delta x$. Suppose the quantity of good X is reduced by a small, marginal quantity, Δx. The resulting change in TU = $\Delta x \star$ MUx (the amount of the reduction in quantity of X times what that amount had added to TU, its MU). In order to keep the level of TU the same (stay on the same indifference curve), the quantity of good Y must increase by an exactly equal offsetting amount; the resulting change in TU = $\Delta y \star$ MUy (the amount of the addition of Y times what that amount adds to TU, its MU) must equal the initial change in TU from the reduction in good X. So, $\Delta y \star$ MUy = $\Delta x \star$ MUx. Rearranging, we get $\Delta y/\Delta x$ = MUx/MUy. We know the slope is negative, so let's take the absolute value. That is, the |slope of the IC| = MRS = MUx/MUy.

EXAMPLE

Owen is attending a special reception hosted by his employer. One of the main events at the reception is a beer and wine tasting, and Owen likes both beverages in moderation (he is not driving and does not work the next day). It is a cash bar (the employer is donating all proceeds to charity, so the prices are high). The price of a small, 4-oz glass of beer is $5 and the price of a 4-oz glass of wine is $7. He has brought $35 with him to spend on beverages and tip the server. Owen knows his total utility for various amounts of beer and wine (and his physical limits—no more than 24 oz in total and he'll be snacking and drinking water in between):

Owen's total utility from glasses of beer or glasses of wine

Quantity	Beer	Wine
1	5	10
2	17	14
3	27	21

How many glasses of beer and glasses of wine should Owen have if he wants to maximize his total utility?

We need to find the marginal utility per dollar spent for each quantity of each beverage.

Quantity	TU Beer	MU Beer	MU/P for Beer	TU Wine	MU Wine	MU/P for Wine
1	5	5	1	10	10	1.4
2	17	12	2.4	24	14	②
3	27	10	②	32	8	1.1

The marginal utilities per dollar spent on beer and wine are equal at a value of 2. These correspond to 3 small glasses of beer and 2 small glasses of wine; this is Owen's optimal consumption bundle of beer and wine. At the given prices, Owen spends $15 on beer and

$14 on wine for a total expenditure of $29 and $6 left to tip the server. We know that Owen is maximizing his total utility, given his budget constraint.

We also know that the |slope of his budget constraint| when beer is on the x-axis is 5/7. If we knew what his indifference curve looked like, we could draw it so it was just tangent to his budget constraint at 3 beer and 2 wine. We know the |slope of the indifference curve| at that point is 5/7, equal to the |slope of his budget constraint|, because he is maximizing his total utility.

KEY TERMS

utility

consumption bundle

marginal utility, MU

diminishing MU

income constraint

price constraint

budget constraint, BC

relative price

opportunity cost

budget set

indifference curve, IC

map

perfect substitutes

perfect complements

marginal rate of substitution, MRS

substitution effect

income effect

SOLVED EXAMPLE PROBLEMS

1. Sheena has a budget of $420 which she can allocate to buying tickets for either Toronto Raptors games or the ballet. The price of a ballet ticket is $60 and the price of a Raptors ticket is $120. Her total utilities from different quantities of events are given in the table below. Use the information in the table to answer the following questions.

# of Events	TU for Ballet Tickets	TU for Raptors Tickets
1	21	60
2	46	100
3	66	130
4	81	150

a) Calculate the MU per dollar spent for ballet and Raptors tickets.

# of Events	TU for Ballet Tickets	MU of Ballet Tickets	MU/P of Ballet Tickets	TU for Raptors Tickets	MU of Raptors Tickets	MU/P of Raptors Tickets
1	21	21	0.35	60	60	0.50
2	46	25	0.416	100	40	0.33
3	66	20	0.33	130	30	0.25
4	81	15	0.25	150	20	0.167

b) How many of each ticket will Sheena purchase to maximize her total utility?

She will purchase where the MU/P on ballet tickets = the MU/P on Raptors tickets. This happens when the MU/P for each are equal to 0.33. These numbers correspond to 3 ballet tickets and 2 Raptors tickets.

c) What is her total utility and how much does she spend?

Sheena's TU = 66 (from the 3 ballet tickets) + 100 (from the 2 Raptors tickets) = 166 utils. She spends 3 * 60 + 2 * 120 = $420.

d) Could she have purchased 3 ballet and 3 Raptors tickets?

Sheena would have to spend 3 * 60 + 3 * 120 = $540 to buy that bundle of tickets. She does not have sufficient income to do so, so the answer is no.

2. Cameron has a budget of $5000 to spend on vacations throughout the year. He loves to ski at Holiday Valley, and a weekend package there costs $250. He also likes to take in the sun in the Dominican Republic; packages there cost $1000 for a week.

a) What is the equation of Cameron's budget constraint?

Let SKI = quantity of ski packages at Holiday Valley and SUN = quantity of Dominican holiday packages. Cameron's budget constraint is

250 * SKI + 1000 * SUN = 5000

b) Draw Cameron's budget constraint.

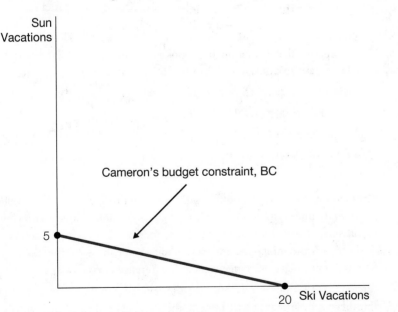

c) What is the slope of Cameron's budget constraint?

The slope is Px/Py = 250/1000 = 0.25. Note that this is the opportunity cost of ski vacations in terms of sun vacations: to get 1 ski vacation, give up 0.25 sun vacations.

d) Suppose Cameron currently has booked 2 sun vacations and 4 ski trips. Is Cameron maximizing his total utility from his holidays?

Cameron is spending 2 * 1000 = 2000 on the Dominican trips and 4 * 250 = 1000 on the Holiday Valley trips for a total of $3000. He's not spending all of his budget so he can't possibly be maximizing his total utility (he has to be *on* his budget constraint in order to be tangent to the highest indifference curve attainable). He has $2000 he can still spend to book more ski and/or sun vacations and reach a higher indifference curve.

Here's what his current consumption looks like. Let's draw a representative indifference curve (since we don't know what his preferences really look like).

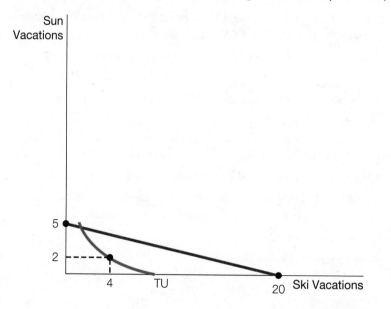

e) Now suppose that Cameron had booked 3 sun holidays. How many ski trips would he have to book in order to potentially maximize his total utility?

Cameron has to spend all of his budget. Then,

$250 \star SKI + 1000 \star SUN = 5000$

$250 \star SKI + 1000 \star 3 = 5000$

$250 \star SKI = 2000$

$SKI = 8$

Cameron would have to book 8 ski trips in order to spend all of his budget and be consuming holidays at a point on his budget constraint. Without knowing what his indifference curves look like, we can't say for sure if this combination of 3 sun and 8 ski trips is the utility-maximizing bundle. You can be on the budget constraint but at a point that's not tangent to an indifference curve.

f) Pretend that Cameron *is* consuming the optimal bundle of sun and ski vacations. Further suppose that at that bundle, the marginal utility of sun vacations is 450. What must be the marginal utility of ski vacations?

At the optimal consumption bundle, $MU_{SKI}/P_{SKI} = MU_{SUN}/P_{SUN}$. We just have to solve for MU_{SKI}.

$MU_{SKI}/250 = 450/1000$

$MU_{SKI} = 112.50$

Notice that the MUs of each vacation aren't equal; it's the MU *per dollar spent* on each that have to be equal.

g) What is the slope of Cameron's indifference curve at the point of tangency?

The |slope| of the indifference curve = the |slope| of the budget constraint. In part c above we calculated the budget constraint |slope| to be 0.25. So, the |slope| of the indifference curve has to be 0.25 as well.

h) Even though we don't know what Cameron's indifference curve looks like, draw a representative curve tangent to the budget constraint at the optimal consumption bundle we solved for in part e.

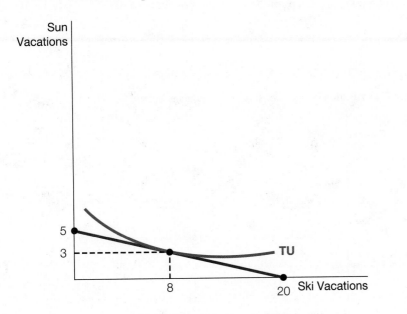

1. Rose collects vintage photo postcards of Canadian towns and sports cards. Postcards sell for $15.00 each on average and sports cards sell for $6.00 each on average. Rose has allocated a budget of $600 annually for her purchases. Let PC = quantity of postcards and SC = quantity of sports cards.

    a) What is the equation of Rose's budget constraint? What is the slope of the budget constraint when postcards are on the horizontal axis?

    b) Draw Rose's budget constraint on the axes below.

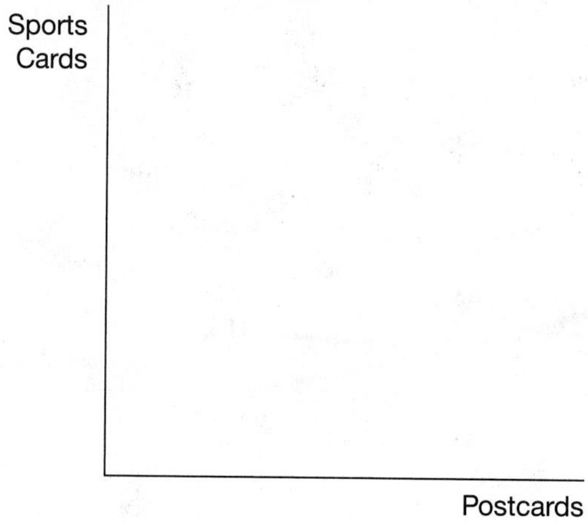

    Sports
    Cards

    Postcards

    c) Suppose Rose is currently purchasing 20 post cards and 40 sports cards. Could this bundle be a possible candidate for utility maximization? Explain.

    d) Suppose Rose were maximizing her total utility by purchasing 30 postcards. How many sports cards would she have to be purchasing in order for her to be consuming a combination that could be a possible optimal bundle?

e) Assume that the bundle you solved for in part d is the optimal consumption bundle. Further suppose the marginal utility of 30 postcards is 40. What must the marginal utility of sports cards equal at the total utility-maximizing bundle?

f) Draw a representative indifference curve to illustrate the optimal bundle from part d.

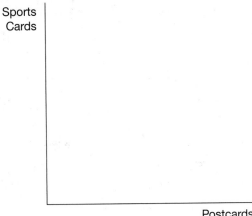

g) The following table reflects everything you've done in parts a to f. Fill it in to confirm the optimal consumption bundle of 30 postcards and 25 sports cards. How do you know it's the optimal bundle?

POSTCARDS				SPORTS CARDS			
Q	TU_{PC}	MU_{PC}	$MU_{PC}/15$	Q	TU_{SC}	MU_{SC}	$MU_{SC}/6$
0	0			0	0		
10	550			10	300		
20	1050			25	460		
30	1450			50	760		
40	1700			100	1060		

2. For each of the following scenarios, sketch a representative indifference curve map with 2 indifference curves. Indicate the direction of increasing total utility.

a) Stephane will always give up 2 hamburgers for 1 double cheeseburger.

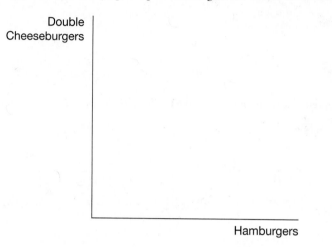

b) Dina receives 100 utils in total utility from an HD TV and a PVR to record her favourite shows. She would be even more satisfied if she had a TV and PVR in every room in her house.

PVRs |

_____
                HD TVs

c) Femi likes pizza and wings but he really likes pizza much better. It would take a lot of wings to get him to give up even a little pizza.

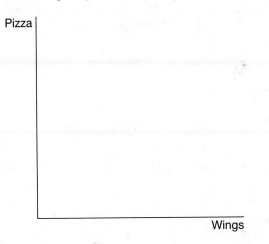

d) Emily also likes pizza and wings, but unlike Femi, she strongly prefers wings to pizza. She'll only give up a little wings and then only if she gets a lot of pizza to compensate.

Pizza

Wings

e) Silvio enjoys both lattes and cappuccino and will trade some of one to get more of the other, but not at a constant rate. (Silvio is our typical consumer with typical preferences.)

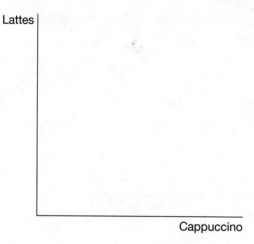

1. Rose collects vintage photo postcards of Canadian towns and sports cards. Postcards sell for $15.00 each on average and sports cards sell for $6.00 each on average. Rose has allocated a budget of $600 annually for her purchases. Let PC = quantity of postcards and SC = quantity of sports cards.

    a) What is the equation of Rose's budget constraint? What is the slope of the budget constraint when postcards are on the horizontal axis?

    15 * PC + 6 * SC = 600

    Slope = Price of postcards/Price of sports cards = 15/6 = 2.5. The budget constraint is negatively sloped but we know this and drop the minus sign.

    b) Draw Rose's budget constraint on the axes below.

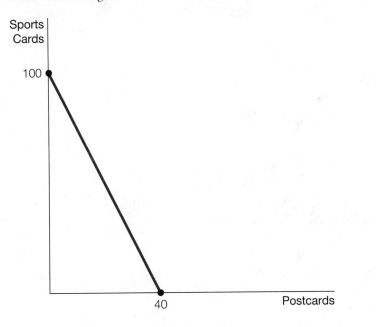

    c) Suppose Rose is currently purchasing 20 post cards and 40 sports cards. Could this bundle be a possible candidate for utility maximization? Explain.

    15 * 20 + 6 * 40 = 540

    Rose is not spending all her income and she's not on her budget constraint; this can't be an optimal consumption bundle because it can't be tangent to the highest possible indifference curve.

    d) Suppose Rose were maximizing her total utility by purchasing 30 postcards. How many sports cards would she have to be purchasing in order for her to be consuming a combination that could be a possible optimal bundle?

    15 * 30 + 6 * SC = 600

    6 * SC = 150

    SC = 25. This quantity will ensure Rose is consuming on her budget constraint.

e) Assume that the bundle you solved for in part d is the optimal consumption bundle. Further suppose the marginal utility of 30 postcards is 40. What must the marginal utility of sports cards equal at the total utility-maximizing bundle?

At the optimal combination, we have the tangency condition $MU_{PC}/P_{PC} = MU_{SC}/P_{SC}$.

$40/15 = MU_{SC}/6$

$MU_{SC} = 16$

Remember, the MU per dollar spent on each good have to be the same, not just the MUs.

f) Draw a representative indifference curve to illustrate the optimal bundle from part d.

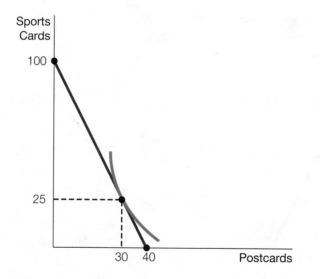

g) The following table reflects everything you've done in parts a to f. Fill it in to confirm the optimal consumption bundle of 30 postcards and 25 sports cards. How do you know it's the optimal bundle?

POSTCARDS				SPORTS CARDS			
Q	TU_{PC}	MU_{PC}	$MU_{PC}/15$	Q	TU_{SC}	MU_{SC}	$MU_{SC}/6$
0	0			0	0		
10	550	55	3.67	10	300	30	5
20	1050	50	3.33	⃝20	460	16	⃝2.67
⃝30	1450	40	⃝2.67	50	760	12	2
40	1700	25	1.67	100	1060	6	1

At the optimal combination, we have the tangency condition $MU_{PC}/P_{PC} = MU_{SC}/P_{SC}$.

$40/15 = 16/6 = 2.67$

Again, remember that the MU per dollar spent on each good have to be the same, not just the MUs.

2. For each of the following scenarios, sketch a representative indifference curve map with 2 indifference curves. Indicate the direction of increasing total utility.

a) Stephane will always give up 2 hamburgers for 1 double cheeseburger.

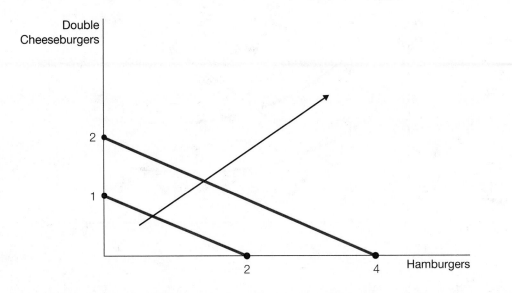

b) Dina receives 100 utils in total utility from an HD TV and a PVR to record her favourite shows. She would be even more satisfied if she had a TV and PVR in every room in her house.

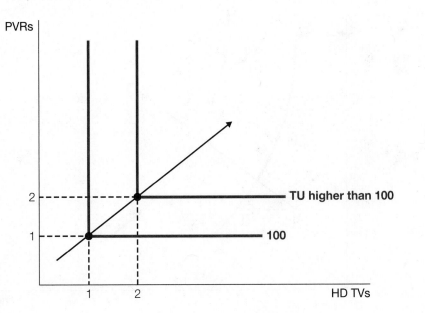

c) Femi likes pizza and wings but he really likes pizza much better. It would take a lot of wings to get him to give up even a little pizza.

Femi's indifference curves will be fairly flat to reflect that he needs a lot of wings to give up even a small amount of pizza.

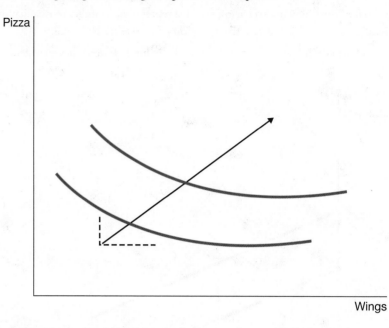

d) Emily also likes pizza and wings, but unlike Femi, she strongly prefers wings to pizza. She'll only give up a little wings and then only if she gets a lot of pizza to compensate.

Emily's indifference curves will be fairly steep to reflect that she will give up a lot of pizza to get even a small amount of wings.

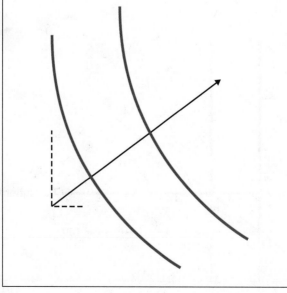

e) Silvio enjoys both lattes and cappuccino and will trade some of one to get more of the other, but not at a constant rate. (Silvio is our typical consumer with typical preferences.)

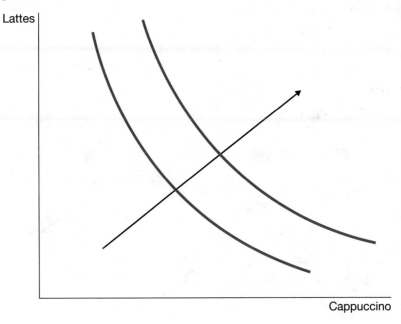

Index